Erich Bulitta, Hildegard Bulitta

Englisch im Alltag – Kompendium

Grundwortschatz, Grammatik, Satzbaumuster, Idiome u.v.m.

GRIN Verlag

Bibliografische Information der Deutschen Nationalbibliothek:

Die Deutsche Bibliothek verzeichnet diese Publikation in der Deutschen National-
bibliografie; detaillierte bibliografische Daten sind im Internet über http://dnb.d-
nb.de/ abrufbar.

Impressum:

Copyright © 2015 GRIN Verlag GmbH
Druck und Bindung: Books on Demand GmbH, Norderstedt Germany
ISBN: 978-3-656-97713-1

Dieses Buch bei GRIN:

http://www.grin.com/de/e-book/300436/englisch-im-alltag-kompendium

GRIN - Your knowledge has value

Der GRIN Verlag publiziert seit 1998 wissenschaftliche Arbeiten von Studenten, Hochschullehrern und anderen Akademikern als eBook und gedrucktes Buch. Die Verlagswebsite www.grin.com ist die ideale Plattform zur Veröffentlichung von Hausarbeiten, Abschlussarbeiten, wissenschaftlichen Aufsätzen, Dissertationen und Fachbüchern.

Besuchen Sie uns im Internet:

http://www.grin.com/

http://www.facebook.com/grincom

http://www.twitter.com/grin_com

Englisch im Alltag

—

Kompendium

Grundwortschatz, Grammatik,
Satzbaumuster, Idiome, ...

Erich und Hildegard Bulitta

Coverbild:
Erich und Hildegard Bulitta

Vorwort

Das Buch „**Englisch im Alltag – Kompendium**" bietet das Grundwissen für Englisch an und ist nicht nur für alle Schülerinnen und Schüler, sondern auch für Erwachsene gedacht, die ihre Schulzeit schon hinter sich haben, ihre Englischkenntnisse (z. B. als Tourist) auffrischen wollen oder Englischkenntnisse für ihren Beruf benötigen. Es bietet in kompakter Form das Englischwissen an, das in der Schule und im Alltag benötigt wird – ohne dass z. B. Grammatik ausführlich bis in alle Einzelheiten behandelt wird. Verständliche Erklärungen und praktische Tipps runden das Angebot ab und erleichtern die Sprachkompetenz.

Das Buch soll allen die Möglichkeit bieten, selbstständig und erfolgreich Englisch zu lernen und im Alltag und in der Schule (z. B. vor Prüfungen) anzuwenden.

Das Buch gliedert sich in fünf Teile:

– **Grundwortschatz mit vielen Zusatzwörtern**
– **Ähnlich klingende Wörter (Homophones)**
– **Englische Redewendungen (Idioms), unregelmäßige Verben**
– **Englische Satzbaumuster**
– **Englische Grammatik (die wichtigsten Regeln)**
– **Übungsteil zum Vertiefen des Wissens**

Dieses Buch kann unabhängig von der Schulart, von eingesetzten Lehrbüchern z. B. in der Volkshochschule, als Sprachschulung oder als Weiterbildungsmaßnahme eingesetzt werden. Es ist ideal, um englischsprachige Länder zu besuchen, wenn Englischkenntnisse aufgefrischt werden sollen. Es enthält eine Zusammenstellung des Englischwissens, das man sowohl für die Schule als auch für den Einsatz im Alltag benötigt.

Da sich das Buch auch an Erwachsene richtet, sind Arbeitsanweisungen in der Höflichkeitsform geschrieben.

Weitere Bücher der Autoren finden Sie im GRIN Verlag. Scannen Sie einfach den QR-Code ein oder besuchen Sie folgende Website:

http://www.grin.com/profile/1095312/#documents

4

Inhalt

Grundwortschatz / Teil 1

Die Wörter in den Kästchen stellen Wörter zu verschiedenen Bereichen dar und sind als Zusatzwortschatz gedacht, auch wenn sie bereits bekannt sind. Ausnahmen bei der Mehrzahlbildung werden aufgeführt. Amerikanische Schreibweisen werden gezeigt.

A

a	einer, eine, eines
able	fähig, kompetent (sein), tüchtig
about	um ... herum, über
account	Bankkonto
ache	Schmerz
in: toothache	Zahnschmerzen
headache	Kopfschmerzen
across	über
active	handelnd, aktiv, tätig
actually	wirklich, tatsächlich
address	Adresse
adult	Erwachsener, erwachsen
advertisement	Inserat, Anzeige
(be) afraid of	sich fürchten (vor)
after	nach
afternoon	Nachmittag
afterwards	nachher
again	wieder
against	gegen
age	Alter, Zeitalter
ago	vor (zeitlich)
in: a year ago	vor einem Jahr
agree	übereinstimmen
air	Luft, Aussehen
airport	Flughafen, Flugplatz
alive	lebendig, am Leben, tätig, unternehmend
all	all, ganz
allow	erlauben, zugestehen
almost	fast, beinahe
alone	allein(e), nur, bloß
along	entlang, längs, weiter
aloud	laut
already	schon, bereits
also	auch, ebenfalls
always	immer(zu), stets
a.m. (auch: am)	vormittags
ambulance	Krankenwagen
and	und
angry	ärgerlich, böse
animal	Tier, tierisch

Schmerzen
backache
cramp
earache
fracture
heart attack
sore throat
sprain
stomach-ache
upset stomach

Tageszeiten
afternoon
evening
lunchtime
midnight
morning
night

Flughafen
airplane
airport
arrival
baggage
declare
departure
distance
flight
fly
land
passenger
pilot
plane
start
steward(ess)

another	ein anderer
answer	Antwort, antworten
any	(irgend)einer, einige, etwas
auch: anyone	einer
anybody	irgendjemand
anyhow	jedenfalls, trotzdem
any more	noch mehr ...?
anyway	irgendwie, sowieso, trotzdem
anything	(irgend)etwas
anywhere	irgendwo(hin), überall
apple	Apfel
appointment	Verabredung, Treffen
army	Heer, Armee
argument	Beweis, Argument
in: have an argument	sich streiten
arm	Arm, Ärmel, dicker Ast
armchair	Sessel, Lehnstuhl
arrival	Ankunft, Eintreffen
arrive	ankommen, eintreffen
art	Kunst, Geschicklichkeit
as ... as	genauso ... wie ...
ashtray	Aschenbecher
ask	fragen, bitten
asleep	schlafend, eingeschlafen
assistant	Mitarbeiter/in, Helfer/in
in: shop assistant	Verkäufer/in
at	an, bei, um, in, für, nach, über, von, zu
at all	überhaupt
at last	endlich
at least	mindestens, wenigstens
at once	sofort, gleich, auf der Stelle
aunt	Tante
autumn	Herbst
away	weg, fort

Früchte
apple
banana
banana
cherry
fruits
gooseberry
grape
lemon
orange
peach
pear
plum
raspberry
strawberry

Great Britain
England
Northern Ireland
Scotland
Wales

B

baby	Baby, Säugling, Kind
back	zurück, Rücken, Rückseite
bad	schlecht, schlimm
bag	Tasche
in: handbag	Handtasche
baggage	Reisegepäck
bake	backen, dörren
baker	Bäcker
balcony	Balkon
ball	Ball
auch: baseball	Baseball
football	Fußball

Haus
ceiling
curtain
door
floor
garden
stairs
wall
wallpaper
window

banana	Banane
bank	Bank, Geldinstitut, Sitzbank
basket	Korb
bath	Bad(ezimmer)
bathing-suit	Badeanzug
bathroom	Badezimmer
be	sein
beach	Strand
bean	Bohne
beautiful	schön, herrlich
because	weil
become	werden
bedroom	Schlafzimmer
beef	Rindfleisch
beer	Bier
before	vor, vorn
beg	bitten (um Verzeihung)
in: I beg your pardon	Entschuldigung! Verzeihen Sie bitte!
begin	anfangen, starten
beginning	Anfang, Start, Beginn
behind	hinter
believe	glauben, vertrauen
bell	Glocke, Klingel, Läuten
belong to ...	gehören zu ...
between	(da)zwischen
big	groß, dick, erwachsen, bedeutend, wichtig
bike (bicycle)	Fahrrad
bill	Rechnung, Plakat, Anschlagzettel, Banknote
bird	Vogel
biro	Kugelschreiber
birth	Geburt, Entstehung, Herkunft, Ursprung
birthday	Geburtstag
biscuit	Keks, Zwieback, Biskuit
bit	bisschen, Stückchen
in: a bit of ...	ein bisschen ...
bitter	bitter, beißend, streng
black	schwarz, dunkel, finster
blanket	Wolldecke, Decke
blood	Blut, Herkunft, Rasse
blouse	Bluse
blow	blasen, stürmen, Schlag
blue	blau, schwermütig
board	Tafel, Brett
boat	Boot, Schiff
body (Pl. bodies)	Körper, Leib, Rumpf
boil	kochen, sieden
bone	Knochen, Gebeine
book	Buch, Heft, Block, buchen, reservieren
boot	Stiefel, Kofferraum
border	Grenze, Kante, Rand

Land
beach
canyon
country
dam
earth
highlands
mountain
National Park
oasis
plateau
sea
State Park

Farben
black
blue
gold
green
grey
pink
red
silver
violet
white
yellow

Körperform
corpulent
female
husky
male
masculine
plump
robust
slender
slim
thick
thin

born	geboren
borrow	entleihen, borgen
both	beide(s)
bottle	Flasche
bottom	Boden, Grund, Ursache
box (Pl. boxes)	Schachtel, Kiste, boxen
in: letterbox	Briefkasten
call-box	Telefonzelle
boy	Knabe, Junge
brake	bremsen, Bremse
bread	Brot
break	Pause, zerstören
breakdown	Panne, Ausfall
breakfast	Frühstück
bridge	Brücke, Steg
bright	hell, leuchtend, klar
bring	(her)bringen, tragen
broad	breit, hell
brother	Bruder
brown	braun
brush	Bürste, Pinsel, bürsten
build	bauen, errichten
building	Gebäude, Bauwerk
bulb	Glühbirne, Knolle
bull	Stier, Bulle
burn	(ver-, an-)brennen
bus (Pl. buses,	
amerik.: busses)	Bus
busdriver	Busfahrer
bus stop	Bushaltestelle
business	Geschäft, Handel
busy	beschäftigt
but	aber
butcher	Metzger, Fleischer
butter	Butter
button	Knopf
buy	kaufen, erwerben
by	an, bei, um, neben

Körper
ankle
arm
ear
elbow
eye
finger
forehead
hand
head
heart
hip
leg
lip
nose
shoulder
skeleton
skin
sole
thumb
tongue
tooth, teeth

Fahrzeug
bus
car
lorry
motor-cycle
scooter
taxi
van
vehicle

C

cabbage	Kohl(kopf)
café	Café
cake	Kuchen, Stück (Seife, Schokolade)
call	rufen, nennen, telefonieren, Ruf, Anruf
camera	Kamera, Fotoapparat
camping site	Campingplatz
can	können, Kanne, Behälter
cap	Mütze, Deckel, Verschluss
capital	Hauptstadt
car	Auto, Wagen
in: car park	Parkplatz
car crash	Unfall
caravan	Wohnwagen, Karawane
cardboard	Pappe
cardigan	Wolljacke
careful	vorsichtig, sorgfältig
carry	tragen, überbringen
cassette recorder	Kassettenrekorder
castle	Schloss, Burg
cat	Katze
cattle	Rind(vieh)
ceiling	Zimmerdecke
cellar	Keller
cemetary	Friedhof
cent	Hundert
in: per cent	Prozent
centimetre	Zentimeter
central heating	Zentralheizung
centre (amerik.: center)	Zentrum, Mitte, Mittelpunkt
century	Jahrhundert
cereal	Getreide
certificate	Zeugnis, Attest, Urkunde
chair	Stuhl, Sitz
chance	Chance, Zufall
change	umziehen, verändern, wechseln, Wechselgeld
cheap	billig, preiswert
check	(über)prüfen, hemmen
cheers	Hochrufe, Jubel, Prost!
cheese	Käse
chemist	Apotheker, Chemiker
cheque	Scheck
cherry	Kirsche
chest	Brust, Kiste, Kasten

Verkehr
bicycle
bike
crash
dangerous
drive
driver
fast
headlight
mountainbike
oil
petrol
repair
slow
speed
start
stop
tyre
wheel
windscreen

Ortschaften
city
town
village

10

chicken	Hühnchen, Huhn, Hähnchen
child (Pl. children)	Kind
chimney	Kamin, Schornstein
chips	Pommes frites
chocolate	Schokolade
choose	(aus)wählen
Christian name	Vorname
Christmas	Weihnachten
church	Kirche, Gottesdienst
cigar	Zigarre
cigarette	Zigarette
cinema	Kino
city (Pl. cities)	Stadt, Geschäftsviertel, Altstadt, Innenstadt
class	Klasse, Gesellschaftsschicht, Qualität
in: classmate	Klassenkamerad
classroom	Klassenzimmer
clean	putzen, sauber, neu, unbenutzt, fehlerfrei
clear	klar, rein, sauber, säubern, (be)reinigen
clever	gescheit, intelligent, klug
climate	Klima, Stimmung
climb	klettern, (empor)steigen
clock	Uhr
auch: alarm clock	Wecker
close	schließen, knapp, eng
clothes	Kleider, Wäsche
cloud	Wolke, Trübung
cloudy	wolkig, trüb, unklar, bewölkt
coach	Reisebus, Trainer
coast	Küste
coat	Mantel, Überzug, Hülle
auch: coat-hanger	Kleiderbügel
coffee	Kaffee
cold	kalt, Kälte, Erkältung
collect	sammeln
colour (amerik. color)	Farbe
comb	kämmen, Kamm
come	kommen, sich belaufen auf
comfortable	bequem, gemütlich
complain	sich beschweren
cook	kochen, Koch, Köchin
cool	kühl, kalt(blütig)
copy	Kopie, Abschrift
corner	Ecke, Winkel, Eckball
correct	verbessern, richtig
corridor	Gang, Flur, Korridor
cost	kosten, Preis, Kosten
cotton	Baumwolle
couch	Couch, Liegesofa, Bett
count	(aus)zählen, rechnen, schätzen, Schätzung
country	Land, Vaterland, Gebiet
course	Lauf, Gang, Kurs

Berufe
baker
bookseller
butcher
chemist
clerk
secretary
teacher

Uhrzeit
... o'clock
a quarter ...
a.m.
after
alarm clock
before
exact
fast
half an hour
half past
hour
late
minute
moment
p.m.
past
quick
ring
second
slow
till
to
watch
wristwatch

in: of course	selbstverständlich
cousin	Vetter, Base, Kusine
cover	zudecken, Deckel
cow	Kuh
cross	überqueren, Kreuz
crossing	Kreuzung
crowd	Menge, Gedränge, Haufen
cry (he cries)	weinen, Schrei
cucumber	Gurke
cup	Tasse, Pokal, Kelch
cupboard	Schrank, Büfett
curtain	Vorhang, Gardine
cushion	Kissen, Polster, polstern, abdecken
customs	Zoll
cut	schneiden, Schnitt

Ausdehnung
dimension
expanse
extensive
frontier
lower part
square
upper part

D

daily	täglich, jeden Tag
dance	tanzen, Tanz
danger	Gefahr
dangerous	gefährlich
dark	dunkel, Dunkelheit
date	Datum, Verabredung
daughter	Tochter
day	Tag
dead	tot
death	Tod
dear	teuer, lieb
declare	verzollen, anmelden
in: anything to ...?	etwas zu verzollen?
deep	tief(sinnig)
degree	Grad (Temperatur)
dentist	Zahnarzt
department store	Kaufhaus, Warenhaus
departure	Abreise, Abfahrt
desk	Pult, Schreibtisch
dessert	Nachtisch
dial	wählen, anrufen
dictionary	Wörterbuch
die	sterben
difference	Unterschied, Differenz
different	verschieden, anders
difficult	schwierig
dining room	Esszimmer
dinner	Mittagessen
direction	Richtung
dirty	schmutzig
dish (Pl. dishes)	Schüssel, Platte
auch: dishwasher	Spülmaschine
distance	Entfernung

Tiere
animal
bird
bull
calf, calves
canary
cat
cattle
chicken
cow
deer
dog
fish
goose, geese
hen
horse
monkey
mouse, mice
ox, oxen
pet
pig
pigeon
rabbit
sheep
turkey

disturb	stören, beunruhigen
do	tun, machen
doctor	Arzt, Doktor
dog	Hund
dollar	Dollar ($)
door	Türe
down	abwärts, unten
downstairs	treppab, (nach) unten
draw	zeichnen
dream	träumen, Traum
dress	sich anziehen, Kleid
dressmaker	Schneider(in)
drink	trinken, Getränk
drive	fahren, Fahrt
driver	Fahrer
driving licence	Führerschein
dry	trocknen, trocken
during	während

Trinken
ale light
beer
chocolate
coffee
empty
get drunk
juice
lemonade
milk
mineral water
punch
soft drink
tea
whisky
wine

E

each	jeder, jede, jedes
ear	Ohr
early	früh, Frühe
earn	verdienen
east	Ost(en), Orient
Easter	Ostern
easy	leicht
eat	essen
egg	Ei
either ... or ...	entweder ... oder
electric	elektrisch
in: electric iron	Elektro-Bügeleisen
electric razor	Elektro-Rasierer
else	sonst
in: what else?	was (sonst) noch?
employment	Beschäftigung
empty	entleeren, leer
end	beenden, Ende
engine	Motor
enjoy	sich freuen (an)
enough	genug
enter	eintreten (in)
entrance	Eintritt
in: (entrance) fee	Eintrittsgeld
envelope	Briefumschlag
escape	entfliehen, Flucht
even	sogar, eben
evening	Abend
ever	jemals, immer
every	jeder, jede, jedes

Feiertage
anniversary
Bank Holiday
birthday
Christmas
Christmas Day
Christmas Eve
Easter
feast
holiday
Labor Day
New Year
New Year's Eve
Thanksgiving Day
wedding
Whitsuntide

Elektrogeräte
cooker
drier, dryer
fridge
iron
radio
record-player
shaver
television set
vacuum cleaner
washing machine

auch: everyone	jeder, alle
everything	jedes, alles
everywhere	überall
exam	Examen, Kontrolle, prüfen, untersuchen
example	Beispiel
in: for example	zum Beispiel
(Abk. e.g.)	z. B.
except	außer, ausgenommen
excited	gespannt, aufgeregt
exciting	aufregend, spannend
excuse	entschuldigen, Entschuldigung
in: excuse me	entschuldigen Sie (bitte)
exit	Ausgang, Ausfahrt
exercise	Übung, Ausübung, körperliche Bewe-gung
auch: exercise book	Übungsbuch
exist	vorhanden sein, existieren, leben
expensive	teuer, kostspielig
explain	erklären, erläutern, verständlich ma-chen
eye	Auge

F

face	Gesicht
factory	Fabrik
fair	blond, fair, gerecht, ziemlich
fair	Volksfest, Messe
fall	fallen
false	falsch
family	Familie
auch: family name	Familienname
far	weit entfernt, fern
fare	Fahrpreis, Fahrgeld
farm	Bauernhof, Farm
farmer	Bauer, Landwirt
fast	schnell
fasten	festmachen, zumachen
fat	dick, Fett, fett(ig)
father	Vater
favourite	Lieblings...
feel	fühlen, empfinden
fellow	Kamerad, Kerl
fetch	holen
fever	Fieber, Erregung

Verwandtschaft

ancestors
baby
brother-in-law
child, children
couple
cousin
daughter
divorce
generation
godfather
godmother
grandfather
grandmother
grandparents
husband
junior to
marriage
married couple
marry
Miss
Mister
Mistress
nephew
niece
parents single
related
relationship
senior to
sister-in-law
son
son-in-law
unmarried
wife, wives

few	wenige, einige
auch: a few	ein paar
field	Feld, Wiese
auch: football field	Fußballplatz
fill	füllen
auch: fill up	voll füllen
fight	bekämpfen, Kampf
film	Film, (ver)filmen
finally	endlich, schließlich, endgültig
find	finden
fine	schön, fein, Geldstrafe
finger	Finger
finish	beenden, Schluss
fire	Feuer, schießen
firm	Firma, fest, hart, beständig, stabil
fish (Sing. + Pl.)	fischen, Fisch(e)
fit	passen
fix	reparieren, befestigen
flat	platt, Etagenwohnung
flight	Flug
floor	Fußboden, Stockwerk
flour	Mehl
flower	Blume
flu (influenza)	Grippe
fly	Fliege, fliegen
fog	Nebel, Umnebelung, Schleier, umnebeln
foggy	nebelig
follow	(ver)folgen, nachgehen
food (Sing. + Pl.)	Nahrung, Speise, Essen, Futter, Lebensmittel
fool	Narr, Dummkopf
foot (Pl. feet)	Fuß (als Maß ca. 30 cm)
for	für, zu, denn
foreign	fremd, ausländisch
foreigner	Fremder, Ausländer(in)
forest	Wald, Forst
forget	vergessen
fork	Gabel
form	Formular, Form, Gestalt
free	frei, unabhängig
freeze	(ge)frieren, erstarren
fresh	frisch, neu, munter
fridge	Eisschrank, Kühlschrank
friend	Freund(in), Bekannte(r)
frighten	erschrecken
from	von, aus, seit, vor
front	Vorderseite
auch: in front of	vorne
frost	Frost, Reif
fruit	Frucht, Obst
fry	braten, backen
full	voll(ständig)
fun	Scherz, Spaß, sich amüsieren/lustig machen

Familie
family
sister
brother
parents
father
mother

Möbel
chair
cupboard
desk
furniture
old-fashioned
modern
sideboard
table armchair
upholstery
wardrobe

funny	komisch, spaßhaft, spaßig, sonderbar
furniture	Möbel, Einrichtung, Ausstattung

G

gale	Sturm, Brise
gallon	Gallone (ca. 4,5 Liter; amerik. 3,78 Liter)
game	Spiel, Scherz, Wild
garage	Garage, Reparaturwerkstatt
garden	Garten
gas	Gas (amerik.: Benzin)
gentleman (Pl. gentlemen)	Herr, feiner Mann
get	erhalten, fassen, machen, gelangen
auch: get up	aufstehen
get on	einsteigen
I get it!	Ich verstehe schon! Ich schaffe es!
get away	wegkommen
get ready	sich fertig machen
girl	Mädchen, Freundin
give	(hin)geben, gewähren
glad	froh, erfreut
glass	Glas
glove	Handschuh
go	gehen, fahren, reisen
God	Gott
gold	Gold
good	gut, tüchtig, günstig
goodbye (amerik.: goodby)	auf Wiedersehen
grandfather	Großvater
grandmother	Großmutter
grass	Gras, Rasen, Weide
great	groß, großartig
green	grün, unreif, unerfahren
greengrocer	Gemüsehändler
grey	grau
grocer	Lebensmittelhändler
groceries	Lebensmittel
ground	Grund(stück), Boden
in: on the ground	auf dem Boden
ground floor	Erdgeschoss
group	Gruppe
grow	wachsen
guess	vermuten, raten, denken
guide	Fremdenführer, führen
gun	Schusswaffe

Religion
angel
apostle
belief in
Bible
bishop
Christ
Christian
church
devil
God
gospel
heaven
hell
Jesus
Lord
our Saviour
paradise
parish
pray
prayer
prophet
religion
religious
the Holy Ghost

H

hair	Haar
auch: hairbrush	Bürste
hair tonic	Haarmittel
hairdo	Frisur
hairdresser	Friseur
half (Pl. halves)	halb, (zur) Hälfte
hammer	Hammer, (ein)hämmern
hand	Hand, aushändigen
happen	geschehen, ereignen
happy	glücklich, zufrieden
hard	hart, schwer, schwierig
hardly	kaum, fast nicht, mit Mühe
hat	Hut
hate	hassen, verabscheuen, nicht mögen, Hass
have (got)	haben, besitzen
he	er
head	Kopf, Vernunft, Verstand, Anführer, Leitung
health	Gesundheit
in: health insurance	Krankenversicherung
hear	(zu)hören, erfahren, erhören
heart	Herz, Gedanken, (das) Innere
auch: by heart	auswendig
heat	heizen, erhitzen, Hitze
heavy	schwer, drückend
help	helfen, Hilfe
here	hier(her), da, jetzt
high	hoch, sehr, mächtig
hill	Hügel, Berg
hit	schlagen, Schlager
hobby	Hobby
hold	halten, Griff
hold-up	Stau, Raubüberfall
hole	Loch, aushöhlen, Höhle
holiday	Feiertag, Ruhetag
holidays (amerik.: vacation)	Ferien, Urlaub
home	Heim, nach Hause
auch: homework	Hausaufgabe
hope	hoffen, Hoffnung
horse	Pferd
hospital	Krankenhaus, Klinik
hot	heiß, scharf, hitzig
hotel	Hotel
hour	Stunde, Zeit(punkt), Uhr
house	Haus
auch: housewife	Hausfrau
how	wie
auch: how much	wie viel?
how long	wie lange?
hungry	hungrig, begierig
hurry	(be)eilen, Eile

Stimmung
cold
cool
feeling
good-natured
happy
mood
sociable
warm

Wetterbericht
bad
change
changeable
chilly
cold
dry
fall
fine
foggy
fresh
hazy
nice
overcast
raining
rainy
shining
stormy
sultry
sunny
temperature
melt
warm
wet
windy

hurt	verletzen, wehtun, kränken, verletzt
husband	Ehemann, Gatte

I

I	ich
ice	Eis
auch: ice-cream	Speiseeis
ice hockey	Eishockey
idea	Idee, Gedanke, Auffassung, Meinung, Ahnung
if	wenn, falls, ob
ill	krank, schlecht, schlimm
illness	Krankheit, Leiden
important	wichtig, bedeutend
impossible	unmöglich
inch	Zoll (= 2,54 cm)
information	Auskunft, Information
in: information bureau	Auskunftsbüro
insurance	Versicherung
insured	versichert
interested (in)	interessiert (an)
interesting	interessant
interview	Interview, Befragung, befragen
into	in, hinein
invite	einladen
it	es

Krankheit
breakdown
cough
disease
influenza
injury
pain
recovery
sickness

J

jacket	Jacke
jam	Marmelade
job	Arbeit, Stellung, Beruf
join	verbinden, treffen
joke	spaßen, Witz, Scherz
journey	Reise
juice	Saft
in: orange juice	Orangensaft
apple juice	Apfelsaft
jump	springen, Sprung
just	richtig, gerade, eben

Beruf(e)
apprentice
apprenticeship
baker
craft
craftsman
hairdresser
printer
workshop

18

K

keep	(be)halten, bewahren
key	Schlüssel
kill	töten, schlachten
kilometre	Kilometer
kind	freundlich, Art, Sorte
king	König, Herrscher
kiss	küssen, Kuss
kitchen	Küche
knee	Knie
knife (Pl. knives)	Messer
knock	klopfen, Schlag
know	wissen

Haushalt
brush
fork
jug
mug
pan
plate
pot
spoon
tray

L

lady (Pl. ladies)	Dame, Lady
lamp	Lampe, Leuchte
land	landen, Boden, Land
last	letzte, dauern
late	(zu) spät
later	später
laugh	lachen, Lachen
lay	legen
in: lay the table	den Tisch decken
lazy	faul
learn	lernen
leave	verlassen
left	links, verlassen (von leave)
leg	Bein
lemonade	Limonade
lend	(ver-, aus-)leihen
let	lassen, gestatten
letter	Buchstabe, Brief
lie	liegen, Lüge, lügen
life (Pl. lives)	Leben
lift	heben, Aufzug
light	leicht, Licht
like	mögen, wie (Vergleich)
line	Zeile
lip	Lippe
auch: lipstick	Lippenstift
listen	lauschen, zuhören
litre (amerik.: liter)	Liter
little	klein, wenig, kurz
live	leben, lebendig, wohnen
living room	Wohnzimmer
lock	absperren, Schloss
long	lang
look	(an)schauen, Blick

Zeit
... ago
afterwards
before
constant
durable
early
eternal
immediately
instantly
late
now
past
previously
sometimes
soon first
suddenly
then
till
today
tomorrow
yesterday

lorry (Pl. lorries)	Lastwagen
auch: lorry driver	Lastwagenfahrer
lose	verlieren, einbüßen
lot	Menge
in: a lot of	eine Menge von
loud	laut
auch: loudspeaker	Lautsprecher
love	lieben,
Liebe	
low	niedrig, tief, seicht, flach, leise,
schwach	
luck	Glück(sfall)
lucky	glücklich
lunch	Imbiss, Mittagessen

Wohnung
(first / second) floor
bathroom room
bedroom
cellar
dining room
flat
hall
kitchen
living room
nursery
restroom
toilet / restroom

M

machine	Maschine
auch: coffee machine	Kaffeemaschine
washing machine	Waschmaschine
make	machen, schaffen, herstellen, anfertigen
man (Pl. men)	Mann
manage	zurechtkommen, es schaffen
many	viele, manche(r, s)
map	Landkarte
market	Markt
marry	heiraten
match	Streichholz, Spiel(abschnitt)
matter	Sache, Ursache
in: what's the matter?	was gibt es?
as a matter of fact	Tatsache
may	können, dürfen
maybe	viel-
leicht	
meal	Mahl-
zeit	
mean	bedeuten, ge-
mein	
meat	Fleisch
auch: cold meat	kalter Bra-
ten	
medicine	Medizin, Arz-
nei	
meet	treffen, zusammenkommen
meeting	Treffen, Zusammenkunft
menu	Speisekarte
metal	Metall, Schotter
meter	Zähler
metre	Meter
middle	Mitte, mittlere(r,s)

Mahlzeit
appetite (for)
breakfast
dinner
fried egg
High Tea
lettuce
lunch
mashed potatoes
meal
pepper
poultry
roast meat
salad
salt
spice
supper
tea time
toast
well done

mile	Meile (= 1,608 km)
milk	Milch, melken
mineral water	Mineralwasser
minute	Minute, Augenblick
mirror	Spiegel
mist	Nebel
mistake	Fehler
mix	(ver)mischen
modern	modern, neu(zeitlich)
moment	Augenblick
money	Geld
month	Monat
moon	Mond
more	mehr, noch, wieder
morning	Morgen
most	meist, höchst, größt
mother	Mutter
motorbike	Motorrad
motorway	Autobahn
mountain	Berg
mouth	Mund(stück), Öffnung
much	viel, sehr
in: how much?	wie viel?
museum	Museum
music	Musik(stück), Noten
must	muss

Musik
flute
guitar
horn
instrument
melody
musician
organ
piano
saxophone
to play the ...
trumpet
violin

N

nail	Nagel, (an)nageln
auch: fingernail	Fingernagel
name	Name
narrow	eng, schmal
near	nahe, vertraut, genau exakt, gegen (Zeit)
nearly	fast, beinahe
neck	Hals, Nacken
auch: necklace	Halskette
need	brauchen, benötigen, Not, Mangel
needle	Nadel
neighbour	Nachbar
never	niemals, durchaus nicht, gar nicht
new	neu, modern, frisch
news (Sing. + Pl.)	Neuigkeit(en), Nachricht(en)
newspaper	Zeitung
next	nächst, zunächst
nice	fein, nett, hübsch
night	Nacht
auch: good night	gute Nacht!
nightdress	Nachthemd
no	kein, nein
auch: no-one	niemand, keiner

Kleidung
blouse
coat
jeans
knitwear
nightdress
pullover
pyjamas
shorts
skirt
stockings
(T-)shirt
trousers
underwear

nowhere	nirgend(s)
noise	Lärm, Geräusch
north	nördlich, Norden
nose	Nase
not	nicht
auch: not at all	durchaus nicht
not either	auch nicht
nothing	nichts
notice	(be)achten, Anzeige
now	jetzt, eben, nun
number	Nummer
auch: number-plate	Nummernschild

O

of	von, aus
off	weg, ab, aus
office	Büro, Geschäftsstelle, Amt
auch: post office	Postamt
lost property office	Fundbüro
often	oft, häufig
oil	Öl
old	alt, erfahren
on	auf, an, bei
once more	noch einmal
one-way street	Einbahnstraße
only	nur, einzig
open	öffnen, offen
opening hours	Öffnungszeiten
opposite	gegenüber(liegend)
or	oder
orange	Orange
order	Befehl, Ordnung, bestellen
ordinary	gewöhnlich, üblich
other	andere(r, s)
out	aus, hinaus, heraus, draußen
outside	Äußere, außen, außerhalb, Außenseite
over	über, vorbei, mehr
own	besitzen, eigen(es, er)
owner	Besitzer, Eigentümer

Straße
bend
cul-de-sac
freeway
highway
interstate
lane
motorway
one-way
pavement
road
street
traffic lights
way
zebra crossing

P

packet	Päckchen, Packung, Schachtel
in: a packet of cigarettes	ein Päckchen Zigaretten
page	Seite
pain	Schmerz, Pein, Kummer
pair	Paar
pan	Pfanne
paper	Papier, Zeitung
parcel	Paket
pardon	Verzeihung
in: I beg your pardon	Entschuldigung!
parents	Eltern
park	parken, Park, Naturschutzgebiet
part	Teil, Stück, Anteil
party	Partei, Partie, Party
pass	vorbeigehen (zeitlich und räumlich), Gebirgspass
passenger	Fahrgast, Passagier, Reisender
passport	Pass, Reisepass
past	vorbei, nach, vergangen
patient	Patient, geduldig
pay	bezahlen
peace	Friede, Ruhe
pear	Birne
pedestrian	Fußgänger
auch: pedestrian precinct	Fußgängerzone
pedestrian crossing	Zebrastreifen
pen	Füller
pencil	Bleistift
penny	Penny, Centstück
people (Sing. + Pl.)	Volk, Leute
perhaps	vielleicht
person	Person
pet	zahmes Tier, Haustier
petrol	Benzin, Treibstoff
auch: petrol station	Tankstelle

Gewässer
lake
loch
ocean
pond
river
sea
stream

Frieden/Streit
armistice
disarmament
hero
invasion
negotiation
occupation
occupy
peace
peaceful
raid
treaty of peace
victor
victorious
war

phone	telefonieren	
photo	Foto	**Post**
pick	pflücken, zupfen	address
auch: pick up	aufheben	answer
picture	Bild	call
picture postcard	Postkarte	card
pie	Pastete, Obstkuchen	e-mail
piece	Stück	envelope
pig	Schwein	letter
picnic	Picknick	letterbox
pill	Pille, Tablette	mail
pillow	Kopfkissen	mailbox
pilot	Pilot	parcel
pin	Reißnagel, Anhefter, anheften	post free
pipe	Pfeife	postage
pity	Mitleid	postcard
in: What a pity!	Wie schade!	receive
It's a pity that ...!	Schade, dass ...!	skype
place	Ort, Platz, Stelle	stamp
plan	planen, Plan	telegraph
plane	Flugzeug, flach, eben	telephone
plant	Pflanze, (ein)pflanzen	WhatsApp
plastic	Plastik, plastisch	
plate	Teller	
platform	Bahnsteig	**Recht**
play	spielen	arrest
please	bitte, zufrieden stellen	court convict
plenty of	eine Menge	criminal
plug	Dübel, verstopfen	debt
p.m. (auch: pm)	nachmittags	fine testify
pocket	Tasche	impose
police	Polizei	jail
auch: policeman	Polizist	judge
police station	Polizeistation	jury
police car	Polizeiauto	law-suit
poor	arm, dürftig	lawyer
pop	Pop	murder
in: pop music	Popmusik	police(man)
popstar	Popstar	prison
pork	Schweinefleisch	prisoner
possible	möglich	punish
post	Post	sheriff
in: postcard	Postkarte	suspect
postman	Postbote	suspicious
post office	Postamt	
pot	Topf	
auch: teapot	Teekanne	
potato	Kartoffel	
pound	Pfund (Gewicht, Währung)	
practical	praktisch	
practice	Praxis, Übung	

practise	(aus)üben, proben
prefer	vorziehen
prepare	vorbereiten
prescription	Rezept, Verordnung (Arznei)
presence	Gegenwart, Anwesenheit
present	Geschenk, Gegenwart (gramm.), anwesend sein, überreichen
press	drücken, Presse
pretty	hübsch, nett
price	Verkaufspreis, Lohn
prison	Gefängnis
prisoner	Gefangene(r)
prize	Preis, Gewinn, Prise
programme	Sendung, Programm
promise	versprechen, Versprechen
proud	stolz, eingebildet
pub	Kneipe, Wirtschaft
pudding	Pudding
pull	zerren, ziehen
pullover	Pullover
pupil	Schüler(in)
purse	Geldbeutel
push	stoßen, treiben
put	setzen, stellen, legen
auch: put on	anziehen
pyjamas	Schlafanzug

Gewichte/Maße

acre	= 40,47 a
barrel	= 159,11 l
foot	= 30,48 cm
gallon	= 3,785 l
inch	= 2,54 cm
mile	= 1,608 km
ounce	= 28,35 g
pound	= 453,59 g
quart	= 0,946 l
stone	= 6,348 kg
ton	= 1016 kg
yard	= 91,44 cm

Kleidung
blouse
costume
dinner jacket
evening dress
jacket
textiles
trousers
waistcoat
wardrobe

Qu

quality	Güte, Eigenschaft
quarter	viertel, Viertel
in: a quarter past nine	um 9:15 Uhr
queen	Königin
question	Frage, befragen
quickly	schnell
quiet	still, ruhig
quite	ganz, recht

Zeiten
a quarter past
a quarter to
half past
hour
minute
... o'clock
second

R

race	Rasse, Rennen, Lauf	
radio	Radio	
railway station	Bahnhof	
rain	Regen, regnen	
raincoat	Regenmantel	
rainy	regnerisch	
read	lesen	
ready	bereit, fertig	
really	wirklich, tatsächlich	
recipe	Rezept, Kochrezept	
record	Schallplatte	
auch: record-player	Plattenspieler	
red	rot	
remember	sich erinnern	
repair	reparieren, Reparatur	
repeat	wiederholen	
reporter	Berichterstatter	
rest	Pause, Ruhe, ausruhen	
restaurant	Restaurant, Speiselokal	
restroom	Toilette	
return	zurückkommen	
rice	Reis	
rich	reich	
ride	reiten, fahren, Runde	
right	rechts, richtig, Recht	
ring	Ring, läuten, Telefonanruf	
ripe	reif	
river	Fluss	
road	Weg, Straße	
in: on the road	auf der Straße	
rock	Felsen, Klippe	
roll	(aus)rollen, schlingern, Brötchen, Donner	
roof	Dach	
room	Zimmer, Raum	
round	rund, ringsum	
rubber	Radiergummi	
rule	Regel, Spielregel, Bestimmung	
ruler	Lineal	
run	rennen, fahren, weglaufen	

Restaurant
bill
breakfast
cafeteria
dessert
dinner
drink
eat
first course
hungry
lunch
meal
menu
pub
restaurant
supper
waiter
waitress

Schule
blackboard
cupboard
desk
education
exercise book
form
headmaster
homework
office
pencil
pupil / student
secretary
teacher
workbook

S

sad	traurig, betrübt, bekümmert, niedergeschlagen
safe	sicher, Safe, Tresor
sail	segeln, Segel

salad	Salat
same (the same)	der-, die-, dasselbe
sand	Sand
sandals	Sandalen
sandwich	belegtes Brötchen
saucer	Untertasse
sausage	Wurst
save	sparen, retten
say	sagen, sprechen
school	Schule
auch: primary school	Grundschule
secondary school	höhere Schule
private school	Privatschule
scissors (Sing. + Pl.)	Schere
sea	Meer
season	Jahreszeit
seat	Sitzgelegenheit
second	Sekunde, zweite(r, s)
secretary	Sekretärin
see	sehen
seldom	selten
self-service	Selbstbedienung
sell	verkaufen
send	senden, schicken
sentence	Satz, Strafe
service	überprüfen, Service, Gottesdienst
shake	schütteln
shall	soll(en), werde(n)
in: I / we shall	ich soll / wir sollen
shampoo	Haarwaschmittel
sharp	spitz, scharf
shave	rasieren
she	sie
sheep (Sing. + Pl.)	Schaf(e)
sheet	Blatt Papier, Betttuch, Tuch
shine	strahlen, polieren
ship	Schiff, mit dem Schiff fahren, verschiffen, versenden
shirt	Hemd
shoe	Schuh
shoot	schießen, Schuss
shop	Geschäft
auch: shoeshop	Schuhgeschäft
bookshop	Buchgeschäft, Buchladen
short	kurz
should	sollte(n), würde(n)
shoulder	Schulter
shout	schreien, Schrei

Geographie
Alps
Atlantic Ocean
English Channel
Irish Sea
Isle
Isle of Skye
Isle of Wight
North Sea
Orkney Islands
Peak District
Snowdonia Highlands
Straits of Dover

Geschäfte
amerik. ...center
baker's
bakery
butcher's
drapery
drugstore
grocery
mall
pharmacy
shopping centre
stationer
supermarket
superstore

show	zeigen, Ausstellung
shower	Dusche, Regenschauer
shut	schließen
sick	krank
side	Seite, Rand
sights	Sehenswürdigkeiten
sightseeing	Besichtigung von Sehenswürdigkeiten
sign	Zeichen
silly	albern, töricht
silver	Silber, silbern
simple	einfach, schlicht
since	seit, seitdem
sing	singen
singer	Sänger(in)
sister	Schwester
sit	sitzen
auch: sit down	sich setzen
size	Größe, Umfang
skin	Haut
skirt	Rock
sky	Himmel
sleep	schlafen, Schlaf
slow(ly)	langsam
small	klein, schwach
smell	riechen, Geruch
smile	lächeln, Lächeln
smoke	rauchen, Rauch
snack bar	Imbisshalle
snow	schneien, Schnee
so	so, also
soap	Seife
socket	Steckdose, Sockel
socks	Socken
soft	weich, leise
soldier	Soldat
some	etwas, einige
auch: someone	jemand
something	etwas
somewhere	irgendwo(hin)
sometimes	manchmal
son	Sohn
song	Gesang, Lied
soon	bald
sorry	traurig, betrübt, bekümmert, Entschuldigung!

Sehenswürdigkeiten

Big Ben
bridge
Buckingham Palace
canyon
castle
chapel
church garden
cliffs
Everglades
Grand Canyon
hall
monument
museum
Niagara Falls
skycraper
theatre
tower
Tower Bridge

Ausdruck

active
attractive
beautiful
beauty
charming
cry
graceful
laugh
nice
smile
striking
weep

sort	Sorte, Art, Weise
in: a sort of ...	so etwas wie ...
sound	klingeln, Geräusch, Schall, Ton
soup	Suppe
south	Süden, südlich
souvenir	Andenken
spare time	Freizeit
speak	sprechen, reden
special	besondere(r, s)
speed	Geschwindigkeit, Eile
spell	buchstabieren
spend	verbringen, ausgeben
spoon	Löffel
sport	Sport, Spiel
spring	Frühling, Feder
Square	viereckiger Platz
in: Trafalgar Square	(Platz in London)
stairs (Sing. + Pl.)	Treppen
stamp	Briefmarke
stand	stehen, stellen
star	Stern, Star (Theater, Film, Musik)
start	beginnen, Anfang, Start
station	Bahnhof
stationer	Schreibwarenhändler
stay	bleiben
steak	Steak
steal	stehlen
step	Stufe, gehen
stick	kleben, Stock
still	noch
stockings	Strümpfe
stomach	Magen, Bauch, Leib
stone	Stein, Edelstein
stop	stoppen, aufhalten, Halt
storm	Sturm, Unwetter
story	Geschichte, Erzählung
stove	Ofen
straight	gerade(wegs), ehrlich
stranger	Fremder, Neuling
street	Straße
strong	stark, kräftig
such	solch(e, r), so
suddenly	plötzlich
sugar	Zucker
suit	Anzug, passen
auch: suitcase	Koffer
summer	Sommer
sun	Sonne
auch: sunshine	Sonnenschein
supermarket	Supermarkt

sprechen
add
affirm
chat(ter)
discuss
exclaim
explain
flatter
implore
lisp
maintain
persuade
publish
speak
utter

Gestirne
cloud
darkness
earth
full moon
heaven
illuminate
moon
new moon
planet
shooting
star
space
star
sun
sunbeam
sunshine

supper	Abendessen
sure	sicher, gewiss
surgery hours	Sprechstunde
surname	Nachname
surprise	überraschen, Überraschung
sweet	Bonbon, Nachspeise, süß
swim	schwimmen
auch: swimming pool	Schwimmbad
swimming trunks	Badehose
switch	schalten
auch: switch on	an-, einschalten
switch off	ausschalten

Gegensätze
dirty - clean
hot/warm - cold
in - out
long - short
on - under
rich - poor
satisfied - hungry
slowly - suddenly
strong - weak

T

table	Tisch
auch: tablecloth	Tischtuch, Tischdecke
table tennis	Tischtennis
tablet	Tablette, Stück (Schokolade, Seife)
take	nehmen, dauern, (weg)bringen
talk	Gespräch, reden, sich unterhalten
tall	groß, lang, hoch
tap	Wasserhahn
tape-recorder	Tonbandgerät
taste	schmecken, probieren (Essen)
taxi	Taxi
auch: taxi-driver	Taxifahrer
tea	Tee
teach	unterrichten, lehren
teacher	Lehrer(in)
team	Mannschaft
tear	zerreißen, Träne
telegram	Telegramm
telephone	Telefon, telefonieren
in: telephone number	Telefonnummer
telephone directory	Telefonbuch
telephone-box	Telefonzelle
television (TV)	Fernsehen
auch: TV set	Fernsehgerät
TV program(me)	Fernsehprogramm
TV serial	Fernsehserie
tell	erzählen, sagen
temperature	Temperatur
tennis	Tennis
terrible	schrecklich
test	prüfen, Test, Prüfung
text	Text
than	als (bei Steigerung)
thank	Dank, danken

Sport
cricket
cup
football
game
professional
race
rugby
score
soccer
tennis

Fernsehen/Radio
broadcast
forecast
microphone
network
news
radio
receive(r)
show
speaker
studio
tape
television (TV)
video-recording

that	jener, welcher, der, dass
the	der, die, das
theatre (amerik.: theater)	Theater
then	dann, damals, denn
there	da, dort, dorthin
thermometer	Thermometer
they	sie (= Mehrzahl)
thief (Pl. thieves)	Dieb
thin	dünn, leicht, mager, knapp
thing	Ding, Sache, Gegenstand
think	meinen, denken
thirsty	durstig
this	diese(r, s)
through	(hin)durch
throw	werfen, schleudern
ticket	Karte, Fahrschein
tie	binden, Krawatte
till	bis
time	Zeit, Mal, Takt
... times	... mal
in: three times	dreimal
timetable	Stundenplan, Fahrplan
tin	Dose, Blechbüchse, Zinn
tired	müde, erschöpft
to	zu, nach, an, in, bis
toast	Toast, Trinkspruch
today	heute
toe	Zehe, Spitze
together	zusammen
toilet	WC, Toilette
tomato (Pl. tomatoes)	Tomate
tomorrow	morgen
tongue	Zunge, Sprache
tonight	heute Abend/Nacht
too	zu sehr, ebenfalls, auch
tooth (Pl. teeth)	Zahn
auch: toothbrush	Zahnbürste
toothpaste	Zahnpasta
top	Spitze, oberster Teil
touch	anrühren, anstoßen
tourist	Tourist, Reisende(r)
towel	Handtuch
tower	Turm

Unterrichtsfächer
biology
chemistry
geography
history
lesson
mathematics
physical education

Zeitraum
age
ancient
century
date
day
eternity
future
hour
long
moment
month
past
period
present
second
short
time
week
year

town	Stadt
auch: town hall	Rathaus
traffic (Sing. + Pl.)	Verkehr
auch: traffic lights	Ampel
train	Zug
tram	Straßenbahn
travel	reisen, Reise
tree	Baum
auch: plum tree	Pflaumenbaum
pear tree	Birnbaum
trouble	Mühe, Sorge, Unruhe
trousers (Sing. + Pl.)	Hose(n)
true	wahr, echt, treu
try	versuchen
auch: try on	anprobieren
turn	drehen, wenden, richten
auch: turn on	andrehen, einschalten
turn off	ausdrehen, abdrehen
tyre	Reifen

Städte
Brussels
Canberra
Cardiff
Cologne
Dublin
Edinburgh
Glasgow
London
Los Angeles
Moscow
Munich
Paris
Rome
Tokyo
Vienna
Washington

U

ugly	garstig, hässlich
umbrella	Regenschirm
uncle	Onkel
under	unten, unter, darunter
underground	Undergrund, U-Bahn, unterirdisch
understand	verstehen, annehmen, auffassen
up	(hin)auf, herauf, empor
upstairs	treppauf, (nach) oben
use	benutzen, Nutzen, Gewohnheit
useful	nützlich, brauchbar
useless	nutzlos, unnütz, zwecklos, unbrauchbar
usually	gewöhnlich, üblich, normalerweise

V

van	Lieferwagen
vegetable	Gemüse
very	sehr, wirklich
view	Aussicht, Sicht, Blick
village	Dorf, Ortschaft
visit	besuchen, Besuch
visitor	Besucher, Gast
voice	Stimme

Gemüse
cucumber
onion
pea
radish
salad
tomato

W

wait	(ab)warten
waiter	Kellner, Ober
waitress	Kellnerin
wake up	aufwachen, wecken
walk	gehen, Spaziergang
wall	Wand, Mauer
wallet	Brieftasche
want	wünschen, wollen
war	Krieg
warm	warm
wash	sich waschen
auch: wash up	abwaschen
wash-basin	Waschbecken
watch	anschauen, beobachten, Uhr
water	Wasser
way	Weg, Art und Weise
we	wir
weak	schwach, lasch
wear	tragen (Kleider)
weather	Wetter
week	Woche
weight	Gewicht
welcome	willkommen
well	nun, wohl, gut
west	westlich, Westen
wet	nass, feucht
what	was? wie? welcher?
wheel	Rad
auch: steering wheel	Lenkrad
when	wann, wenn, als
where	wo? wohin?
whether	ob
which	welcher, der, die (im Relativsatz)
while	während
white	weiß (Farbe)
who	wer, der, die (im Relativsatz)
why	warum?
wide	weit, breit
wife (Pl. wives)	Ehefrau
wild	wild, toll
will	Wille, Testament, sein (Zukunft)
win	gewinnen, Sieg
wind	Wind
window	Fenster
wine	Wein
winter	Winter
wish	wünschen, Wunsch
with	mit
without	ohne
woman (Pl. women)	Frau, weiblich

Wasser
beach
brook
ford
oasis
river
sea
straits
stream
tides
waterfall

Wetter
air drop(ping)
atmosphere
climate
climate
cloudburst
dry
fog(gy)
forecast
frost
hail
heat snow
hurricane
lightning
moisture
rain
shower
thunder
thunderstorm
tornado
warmth
wet

wonder	sich wundern, Wunder, Verwunderung
in: I wonder where	... wo
I wonder why	... warum
I wonder when	... wann
wonderful	wunderbar
wood	Holz, Wald
word	Wort
work	arbeiten, Arbeit
world	Welt
worry	sich quälen, plagen
in: don't worry	mach' dir nichts draus!
worried	besorgt, beunruhigt
would	würde, wollte
wound	verletzen, Wunde
write	schreiben
wrong	falsch, Unrecht

Verhalten
bore
boring
dislike
distrustful
furious
hate
horrible
insult
love
nasty
proud
restless
worrying

Y

yard	Yard (= 0,9 m)
year	Jahr
yellow	gelb
yes	ja
yesterday	gestern
auch: the day before	
yesterday	vorgestern
you	du, ihr, Sie, man
young	jung, Junge

Zeiten
ancient
antique
future
modern
new
old
past
present

Z

| zero | Null |
| zoo | Zoo, Tiergarten |

Rechtschreibung nach: Collins Dictionary, Harper Collins Publishers, Glasgow

Grundwortschatz / Teil 2

Wochentage: (days of a week)   **Monate:** (months)   **Jahreszeiten:** (seasons)

Monday	mondays	January	
Tuesday	tuesdays	February	
Wednesday	wednesdays	March	spring
Thursday	thursdays	April	
Friday	fridays	May	
Saturday	saturdays	June	summer
Sunday	sundays	July	
		August	
		September	autumn, fall
		October	
		November	
		December	winter

Himmelsrichtungen: west – east – north – south

Feiertage / Festtage: Christmas/Christmas Eve, New Year's Eve, New Year, Easter, birthday, holiday, marriage

Erdteile: Africa – America – Asia – Australia – Europe – Antarctic

Länder – Sprachen – Personen

America	American / English	Ireland	English / Irish / Gaelic
Australia	English	Italy	Italian
Austria	German	Japan	Japanese
Bavaria	German	Mexico	Spanish
Belgium	French / Flemish / Walloon	Morocco	Arabic / French
Canada	English / French	Namibia	German / English
China	Chinese	Netherlands	Dutch
Denmark	Danish	New Zealand	English
Egypt	Arabic	Norway	Norwegian
England	English	Portugal	Portuguese
France	French	Russia	Russian
Germany	German	Scotland	English / Gaelic / Scot(tish)
Great Britain	English	Spain	Spanish
Greece	Greek	Sweden	Swedish
Greenland	Danish	Switzerland	German / Italian / French
Holland	Dutch	Turkey	Turkish
Hungary	Hungarian	Wales	English / Gaelic

British, Bavarian, American, Irish(man), Gaelic, Welsh, German, Scotswoman / Scotsman, Swiss, Namibian, Moroccan, Austrian, Egyptian, Australian, Belgian, Mexican.

Im Übungsteil am Ende gibt es dazu eine Übung.

Zahlwörter

Grundzahlen

eins, zwei, drei, usw.

Ordnungszahlen

erste, zweite, dritte, vierte, usw.

0	null, zero, nought		
1	one	first	**Besonderheiten**
2	two	second	
3	three	third	(... mal)
4	four	fourth	once
5	five	fifth	twice
6	six	sixth	three times
7	seven	seventh	four times
8	eight	eighth	five times
9	nine	ninth	.... times
10	ten	tenth	
11	eleven	eleventh	
12	twelve	twelfth	**Bruchzahlen**
13	thirteen	thirteenth	
14	fourteen	fourteenth	½ one half
15	fifteen	fifteenth	$1/3$ one third
16	sixteen	sixteenth	¼ one fourth
17	seventeen	seventeenth	$1/5$ one fifth
18	eighteen	eighteenth	$1/6$ one sixth
19	nineteen	nineteenth	$1/100$ one hundredth
20	twenty	twentieth	$2/3$ two thirds
21	twenty-one	twenty-first	¾ three quarters/
22	twenty-two	twenty-second	three fourths
23	twenty-three	twenty-third	$2/5$ two fifths
30	thirty	thirtieth	
40	forty	forthieth	
50	fifty	fiftieth	
60	sixty	sixtieth	
70	seventy	seventieth	
80	eighty	eightieth	
90	ninety	ninetieth	
100	one hundred	hundredth	
101	one hundred and one	hundred and first	
102	one hundred and two	hundred and second	
200	two hundred	two hundredth	
300	three hundred	three hundredth	
1000	one thousand	thousandth	
10 000	ten thousand	ten thousandth	
1000 000	million	millionth	

Das englische Zahlwort „milliard" entspricht dem amerikanischen Wort „billion". In der Alltagssprache wird in Großbritannien aber bereits das amerikanische "billion" für das deutsche Wort „Milliarde" verwendet.

Vervielfältigungszahlen		Dezimalzahlen	
einfach	single	1.1	one point one
zweifach	double		
dreifach	threefold, treble, trible	**Gemischte Zahlen**	
vierfach	fourfold, quadruple		
fünffach	fivefold	1½	one and a half
hundertfach	(one) hundredfold	2½	two and a half

Datum / Jahreszahlen im Englischen und Amerikanischen

1. Die Aussprache der Jahreszahl (*and* wird meistens weggelassen)

Schreibweise	Aussprache	
1800	*eighteen hundred*	
1900	*nineteen hundred*	
2000	*two thousand*	
2001	*two thousand (and) one*	*oder: twenty-one*
2002	*two thousand (and) three*	*oder: twenty-two*
2015	*two thousand (and) fifteen*	*oder: twenty-fifteen*

2. Schreibweise und Aussprache des Datums im Britischen Englisch
Grundregel: Tag – Monat – Jahr

		Tag		Monat	Jahr
Man schreibt:		1st		March,	2010
Man sagt:	the	first	of	March	twenty ten

Die zwei Buchstaben nach der Zahl und auch das Komma werden oft weggelassen.

3. Schreibweise und Aussprache des Datums im Amerikanischen Englisch
Grundregel: Monat – Tag – Jahr

	Monat	Tag	Jahr
Man schreibt:	January	1st,	2010
Man sagt:	January	(the)* first	twenty ten

* Beim Sprechen kann der Artikel *the* auch weggelassen werden.

4. Beispielsätze und die korrekten Präpositionen:

I was born in 1999. (Steht die Jahreszahl alleine, dann steht *in*.)
I was born in May. (Steht der Monat alleine, dann steht *in*.)
I was born on 14th March, 2002. (Beim vollständigen Datum steht *on*.)

5. Besonderheiten

An Stelle des Monats steht oft nur eine Zahl. Der 13. März 2010 wird auch so geschrieben:

Britisches Englisch	Amerikanisches Englisch
13-3-2010	3-13-2010
13/3/2010	3/13/2010
13.3.2010	3.13.2010

Gegenwörter (Opposites)

about	exactly	to begin	to finish, to end, to stop
above	below	behind	in front of
absence	presence	below	above
abundance	lack	better	worse
to accept	to refuse	beautiful	ugly
active	lazy, passive	big	small
activity	passivity	birth	death
to add	to subtract	bitter	sweet
to admit	to deny	black	white
adult	child	boring	interesting, exciting
adults	children	to borrow	to lend
advanced	elementary	bottom	top
after	before	boy	girl
against	for	broad / wide	narrow
to agree	to refuse	brother	sister
alike	different	to build	to destroy
alive	dead	to buy	to sell
all	none	careful	careless
always	never	ceiling	floor
to allow	to forbid	certainly	probably
already	not yet	cheap	expensive
always	never	children	parents
amateur	professional	clean	dirty
to amuse	to bore	clever	stupid
ancient	modern	closed	open
ancestor	descendant	cold	hot
angel	devil	come	go
animal	human	comedy	drama, tragedy
to annoy	to satisfy	constant	changeable
answer	question	to continue	to interrupt
to answer	to ask	correct	false, wrong
apart	together	to damage	to repair
approximately	exactly, correct	dangerous	safe
to argue	to agree	daughter	son
arrival	departure	dawn	dusk
to arrive	to depart, to leave	day	night
artificial	natural	dead	alive
to ask	to answer	to defend	to attack
asleep	awake	to deny	to admit
to attack	to defend	to depart	to arrive
autumn	spring	departure	arrival
awful	nice, pleasant	devil	angel
back	in front of	to die	to live
background	foreground	difficult	easy
backward	forward	dirty	clean
bad	good	to divorce	to marry
bad luck	good luck	divorced	married
before	after	domestic	foreign

down	up	to like	to hate
downstairs	upstairs	to live	to die
early	late	long	short
east	west	to lose	to win; to find
easy	difficult, hard	loud	quiet
to emigrate	to immigrate	major	minor
emigration	immigration	man	woman
empty	full	minimum	maximum
to end	to begin	moon	sun
enemy	friend	more	less
to enter	to leave	natural	artificial
entrance	exit	nephew	niece
evening	morning	new	old
everybody	nobody	night	day
everything	nothing	no	yes
excited	calm	normal	strange
export	import	north	south
far	near	occasionally	frequently
fast	slow	off	on
female	male	old	new, modern, young
few	many	other	same
to find	to lose	out	in
finish	start	outside	inside
foreign	domestic	peace	war
foreigner	native	to permit	to forbid
fortune	bad luck	poor	rich, wealthy
friend	enemy	poverty	wealth
future	past, present	to pull	to push
gentleman	lady	rear	front
happy	sad	to reply	to ask
to harvest	to plant	reply	question
health	disease, illness	safe	dangerous
heaven	hell	shallow	deep
here	there	to shut	to open
horizontal	vertical	sometimes	often
host	guest, visitor	summer	winter
huge	tiny	sunny	cloudy, rainy
hungry	thirsty	together	apart
husband	wife	tomorrow	yesterday
inside	outside	true	false
junior	senior	useful	useless
last	first	west	east
late	early	winter	summer
to learn	to teach	woman	man
left	right	yes	no
to lend	to borrow	yesterday	tomorrow
less	more	young	old
life	death		

Vergleich: Amerikanisch – Englisch

Amerikanisch	Englisch	Deutsch
accelerator / gas pedal	accelerator	Gaspedal
aerial / antenna	aerial (TV, radio)	Antenne
after	past	nach (Zeit)
apartment	flat	Wohnung
baggage	luggage	Gepäck
ball-point pen	biro	Kugelschreiber
billion	milliard	Milliarde
block	block of buildings	Häuserblock
busy	engaged	besetzt (Telefon)
call/phone	phone	telefonieren
campus	college ground	Universitätsgelände
can	tin	Konservendose
candy	sweets	Süßigkeiten
catalog	catalogue	Katalog
center	centre	Zentrum
check	bill	Rechnung (Restaurant)
closet	cupboard/wardrobe	Wandschrank
color	colour	Farbe
cookie	biscuit	Keks
cop	policeman (bobby)	Polizist
corn	maize	Mais
cozy	cosy	gemütlich
date	appointment	Termin, Verabredung
daylight saving time	summertime	Sommerzeit
detour	diversion	Umleitung
downtown, city center	city centre	Stadtzentrum
driver´s license	driving licence	Führerschein
drugstore	chemist's	Drogerie
eggplant	aubergine	Aubergine
elevator	lift	Fahrstuhl
erasor	rubber	Radiergummi
expiration date	expiry date	Verfallsdatum
facility manager	caretaker	Hausmeister
fall	autumn	Herbst
favorite	favourite	Lieblings...
fire department	fire brigade	Feuerwehr
first floor	ground floor	Erdgeschoss
first name	Christian name	Vorname
fish-sticks	fish-fingers	Fischstäbchen
to fix	to repair	reparieren
flashlight	torch	Taschenlampe
flavor	flavour	Geschmack, Aroma
freeway / interstate	motorway	Autobahn
French fries	chips	Pommes frites

garbage can / trash can	bin, dustbin	Mülleimer
grade	class/form	Klassenstufe
gas	petrol	Benzin
ground floor, first floor	ground floor	Erdgeschoss, Parterre
grain	corn	Getreide
guy	fellow	Bursche, Kerl
harbor	harbour	Hafen
hi! / howdy!	hallo!	Hallo (Begrüßung)
hood	bonnet	Kühlerhaube
humor	humour	Humor
inquiry	enquiry	Erkundigung
jacket, parka	anorak	Anorak
kids	children	Kinder
last name	surname	Familienname
lawyer, attorney	barrister, solicitor	Rechtsanwalt
mail	post	verschicken (Brief)
Men´s Room	Gents	Herren (Toilette)
movie	cinema	Kino
movie, film	film	Film
motorhome/camper	dormobile	Campingbus
Native American	American Indian	Indianer
one way ticket	single ticket	Fahrkarte (einfach)
on the weekend	at the weekend	am Wochenende
parking lot	car park	Parkplatz
period	full stop	Punkt (Satzzeichen)
potato chips	chrisps	Kartoffelchips
railroad	railway	Eisenbahn
to rent	hire	mieten (Auto)
restroom	lavatory	Toilette
Santa Claus	Father Christmas	Weihnachtsmann
second floor	first floor	1. Etage
sidewalk	pavement	Gehsteig
soccer	football	Fußball
sticker	label	Aufkleber, Anhänger
swimsuit	(bathing) costume	Badeanzug
store	shop	Geschäft
stove	cooker	Küchenherd
streetcar	tram	Straßenbahn
subway	underground/Tube	U-Bahn
theater	theatre	Theater
track	platform	Bahnsteig
trail	path	Spazier-/Wanderweg
trailer	caravan	Wohnwagen / Anhänger
truck	lorry	Lastwagen
trunk	boot	Kofferraum
two weeks	fortnight	14 Tage, zwei Wochen
vacation	holiday	Ferien, Urlaub
yard	garden	Garten (Haus)
zip code	postcode	Postleitzahl

Vergleich: Australisch – Englisch

Australisches Englisch	Britisches Englisch	Deutsch
ace	excellent	toll
aggro	aggressive	aggressiv
Alf	stupid person	doofer Mensch
amber (fluid)	beer	Bier
arvo	afternoon	Nachmittag
Aussie	Australian	Australier
Bickie	biscuit	Keks
billabong	waterhole	Wasserloch
Billie	tea kettle	Teekessel
booze	alcohol	Alkohol
Bottle Shop	Liquor Shop	Alkoholladen
bushranger	criminal	Verbrecher
chokkie	chocolate	Schololade
Chrissie	Christmas	Weihnachten
comfort station	toilet / restroom	Toilette
digger	soldier	Soldat
dill	idiot	Blödmann, Trottel
G'day	Hallo, Hi	Guten Tag, Hallo
gum tree	Eucalyptus tree	Eukalyptusbaum
kiwi	New Zealander	Neuseeländer
mozzie	mosquito	Stechmücke
nana	banana	Banane
pissed	drunk	betrunken
postie	postman	Postbote
Roo	kangaroo	Känguru
snag	sausage	Würstchen
tea	evening meal	Abendbrot
tucker	food	Essen
vegies	vegetables	Gemüse
Yank	American	Amerikaner

Vokabeln im Geschäftsenglisch

Commercial English	Deutsch
accordance (in accordance with)	in Übereinstimmung mit, gemäß
account	Konto
accounting error	Buchungsfehler
acknowledge (to)	anerkennen, zugeben, bestätigen
address	Adresse
addressee	Empfänger
in advance	im Voraus
advance payment	Vorauszahlung
advice of payment	Zahlungsmitteilung
after-sales service	Kundendienst
agreement	Abkommen, Übereinkunft
air freight	Luftfracht
air waybill	Luftfrachtbrief
amount due	fälliger Betrag
apology	Entschuldigung
to apply for	sich bewerben (um)
(on) approval	zur Ansicht
balance	Saldo, Guthaben
bank account	(Bank) Konto
bill of exchange	Wechsel
bill of lading	Frachtbrief
blank cheque	Blankoscheck
branch	Filiale, Zweigstelle
brand	(Firmen-) Marke
buyer	Käufer
cancel	streichen, absagen, rückgängig machen
cargo	Fracht
carriage free	frachtfrei
carriage paid	frei Haus
draft	Wechsel
due date	Fälligkeitsdatum
duty free	zollfrei
enclosed	in der Anlage, anbei, beigefügt
to enclose	beifügen
enquiry	Anfrage
exchange rate	Wechselkurs
expenses	Spesen
extension of payment time	Zahlungsaufschub
failure to pay	Zahlungsunfähigkeit
fee	Honorar, Zahlung, Gebühr
firm offer	verbindliches Angebot
free of charge	kostenlos, umsonst
goods	Waren
to grant a discount	einen Rabatt gewähren

hereby	hiermit
included	inbegriffen
initial order	Erstbestellung
inquiry	Anfrage
insurance	Versicherung
invoice	Rechnung
to invoice	in Rechnung stellen
leaflet	Broschüre
liable	haftbar
money order	Geldanweisung
to negotiate	verhandeln (über etwas)
net price	Nettopreis
opportunity	Gelegenheit
order	Bestellung
to order	bestellen
orderform	Bestellschein
overdue	überfällig
overdrawn	überzogen (Konto)
to postpone	verschieben
preferential rate	Vorzugspreis
profit margin	Profitspanne
purchase	Kauf
purchase	kaufen
quarterly	vierteljährlich
quotation	Kostenvoranschlag
to quote a price	einen Preis angeben
rate	Preis, Tarif
receipt	Rechnung, Quittung
to recommend	empfehlen
refund	rückerstatten
registered letter	Einschreiben
reimbursement	Rückerstattung
repeat order	Nachbestellung
on request	auf Anfrage
requirement	Anforderung, Bedingung
retail price	Ladenpreis
reward	Belohnung
sample	Muster
to ship	versenden, verschiffen
to sign	unterzeichnen
in storage	auf Lager
terms	Bedingungen
valid	gültig
value	Wert
waybill	Frachtbrief
wholesale	Großhandel

Unregelmäßige englische Verben

Im Englischen wird in der Vergangenheit normalerweise beim Verb die Endung **-ed** angehängt wird. Die Ausnahmen dazu sind die unregelmäßigen Verben. Die Hilfsverben wurden in dieser Liste ebenfalls mit aufgenommen. Das Mittelwort der Vergangenheit wird mit **have** / **has** (present perfect) bzw. **had** (past perfect) verwendet.

(*) deutet an, dass das Verb auch in regelmäßiger Form mit der Endung *-ed* vorkommt.

Grundform	Einfache Vergangenheit	Mittelwort der Vergangenheit	
be	was, were	been	sein
beat	beat	beaten	schlagen
become	became	become	werden
begin	began	begun	anfangen, beginnen
bite	bit	bitten	beißen
blow	blew	blown	blasen
break	broke	broken	brechen, kaputtmachen
bring	brought	brought	(her)bringen
build	built	built	bauen
burn (*)	burnt	burnt	brennen
buy	bought	bought	kaufen
catch	caught	caught	fangen
choose	chose	chosen	(aus)wählen
come	came	come	kommen
cost	cost	cost	kosten
creep	crept	crept	kriechen
cut	cut	cut	schneiden
dig	dug	dug	(aus)graben, umgraben
do	did	done	tun, machen
draw	drew	drawn	zeichnen
dream (*)	dreamt	dreamt	träumen
drink	drank	drunk	trinken
drive	drove	driven	fahren, treiben
eat	ate	eaten	essen
fall	fell	fallen	fallen
feed	fed	fed	füttern
feel	felt	felt	sich fühlen
fight	fought	fought	(be)kämpfen
find	found	found	finden
fly	flew	flown	fliegen
forbid	forbad(e)	forbidden	verbieten
forget	forgot	forgotten	vergessen
forgive	forgave	forgiven	vergeben
freeze	froze	frozen	(ge)frieren
get	got	got	werden, bekommen
give	gave	given	geben

go	went	gone	gehen
grow	grew	grown	wachsen, gedeihen
hang	hung	hung	(auf)hängen
have	had	had	haben
hear	heard	heard	hören
hide	hid	hidden	sich verstecken
hit	hit	hit	schlagen, treffen
hold	held	held	halten
hurt	hurt	hurt	verletzen
keep	kept	kept	(be)halten
know	knew	known	kennen, wissen
lay	laid	laid	legen
lead	led	led	führen, leiten
learn (*)	learnt	learnt	lernen, erfahren
leave	left	left	(ver)lassen
lend	lent	lent	(aus)leihen
let	let	let	(zu)lassen
lie	lay	lain	liegen
light	lit	lit	anzünden
lose	lost	lost	verlieren
make	made	made	machen
mean	meant	meant	bedeuten, meinen
pay	paid	paid	bezahlen
put	put	put	setzen, stellen, legen
read	read	read	lesen
ride	rode	ridden	reiten, fahren (Rad)
ring	rang	rung	anrufen, klingeln
rise	rose	risen	aufstehen, aufgehen (Mond)
run	ran	run	rennen, laufen
say	said	said	sagen
see	saw	seen	sehen
sell	sold	sold	verkaufen
send	sent	sent	senden, schicken
set	set	set	stellen, setzen
sew (*)	sewed	sewn	nähen
shake	shook	shaken	schütteln
shine	shone	shone	scheinen
shoot	shot	shot	schießen
shut	shut	shut	schließen
sing	sang	sung	singen
sink	sank	sunk	sinken (Schiff)
sit	sat	sat	sitzen
sleep	slept	slept	schlafen
smell	smelt	smelt	riechen
speak	spoke	spoken	sprechen
spell (*)	spelt	spelt	buchstabieren
spend	spent	spent	ausgeben, verbringen (Ferien)
spring	sprang	sprung	springen
stand	stood	stood	stehen
steal	stole	stolen	stehlen

stick	stuck	stuck	kleben, anstecken
swim	swam	swum	schwimmen
swing	swung	swung	schwingen, schwenken
take	took	taken	nehmen
teach	taught	taught	unterrichten, lehren
tear	tore	torn	(zer)reißen
tell	told	told	(es) sagen, erzählen
think	thought	thought	denken, glauben, meinen
throw	threw	thrown	werfen
understand	understood	understood	verstehen
wake (*)	woke	woke(n)	aufwachen, wecken
wear	wore	worn	anhaben, tragen (Kleidung)
weep	wept	wept	weinen
win	won	won	gewinnen
write	wrote	written	schreiben

Ähnlich klingende Wörter (Homophones)

Immer wieder kommt es zu Verwechslungen von Wörtern, die zwar gleich oder ähnlich ausgesprochen, aber unterschiedlich geschrieben werden. Die folgenden Wörter helfen Ihnen insbesondere beim Diktat. Lesen Sie die Wörter laut vor, prägen Sie sich dabei Aussprache und unterschiedliche Schreibweise ein und wenden Sie die Wörter dann in sinnvollen Sätzen an.

fair	schön, anständig, blond, Messe, Jahrmarkt, gerecht ziemlich, ganz, fair, sonnig	**past**	vergangen, gewesen, Vergangenheit
fare	Fahrgeld, Kost	**passed**	vorübergegangen, vorbei (von: pass)
brake	Bremse, bremsen, Unterholz	**eye**	Auge
break	brechen, Pause, Bruch	**I**	ich
hour	Stunde	**dear**	lieb, teuer, süße(r)
our	unser	**deer**	Rotwild
be	sein	**farther**	weiter
bee	Biene	**father**	Vater, Pfarrer
blew	blasen (von: blow)	**fir**	Fichte, Tanne
blue	blau	**fur**	Pelz
higher	hoch (von: high)	**caught**	fing (von: catch)
hire	(an)mieten	**court**	Gericht, Hof
male	männlich	**hear**	hören
mail	Post, versenden, abschicken	**here**	hier, da
knows	er/sie kennt (von: know)	**meat**	Fleisch
nose	Nase	**meet**	treffen
in	in (Verhältnisort)	**know**	kennen, wissen
inn	Gasthaus, Wirtschaft	**no**	nein, kein
made	machte, gemacht (von: make)	**not**	nicht
maid	Mädchen, Magd	**knot**	Knoten
pair	Paar	**read**	las (von: read)
pear	Birne	**red**	rot (Farbe)
haul	ziehen, zerren, befördern	**great**	groß(artig), mächtig
hall	Halle, Flur, Saal	**grate**	kratzen, reiben, raspeln
some	irgendein, einige, etwas	**sail**	segeln, Segel
sum	Summe	**sale**	Ausverkauf, Verkauf

board	Brett, Kost, Bord	**to**	um, zu, nach
bored	gelangweilt, ausgehöhlt,	**two**	zwei
	(von: bore)	**too**	auch, gleichfalls

buy	kaufen	**ridge**	Rippe, (Dach-)First,
by	durch, von, bei		Bergrücken, Grat
(good)bye	leb(e) wohl	**rich**	reich, wohlhabend

cellar	Keller, einkellern	**whether**	ob
seller	Verkäufer	**weather**	Wetter

plain	klar, einfach, deutlich,	**rain**	Regen, regnen
	einfarbig, uni, Ebene	**reign**	regieren, herrschen,
plane	Flugzeug, Stufe, Ebene,		Regierungszeit,
	flach, eben, Hobel, hobeln,		Amtszeit
	planieren, glätten	**rein**	Zügel, zügeln

sea	Meer	**sees**	sieht (von: see)
see	sehen	**seize**	ergreifen, packen

hurt	verletzen, verletzt(e)	**tin**	Zinn, Konservendose
heard	hörte (von: hear)	**ting**	Klang, klingen

dog	Hund, Rüde, Kerl	**device**	Gerät, Vorrichtung,
doc	Doktor (umgangssprachlich)		Trick, Kunstgriff
dock	Dock, Kai, Hafen, docken,	**devise**	sich ausdenken, vermachen,
	Anklagebank, anlegen, kürzen		hinterlassen

site	Lage, Platz, Gelände	**week**	Woche
sight	Sicht, Anblick	**weak**	schwach, kränklich

hole	Loch, Lücke, Öffnung, Höhle,	**knew**	kannte, wusste
	Bau, schwierige Situation		(von: know)
whole	ganz, heil	**new**	neu

tale	Erzählung, Geschichte, Lüge	**were**	war(en)
tail	Schwanz, Schweif, Ende	**where**	wo?

clock	Uhr	**flour**	Mehl
clog	(Holz-) Klotz, Hindernis	**flower**	Blume

peace	Frieden	**knight**	Ritter
piece	Stück	**night**	Nacht

would	wollte	**rhyme**	Reim, Gedicht
wood	Holz(fass), Wald	**rime**	(Rau-)Reif

pane	Fensterscheibe	**through**	(hin)durch
pain	Schmerz(en), Leid(en)	**threw**	warf (von: throw)

right	richtig, recht, Recht	**sow**	säen, legen
rite	Brauch, Ritus	**sew**	nähen, zunähen
write	schreiben	**so**	so (sehr), dermaßen
ride	fahren, reiten	**though**	obgleich, wenn auch
thrown	geworfen (von: threw)	**bear**	Bär, grober Klotz
throne	Thron	**bare**	nackt, bloß, kahl
flee	(ent)fliehen, flüchten	**altar**	Altar
flea	Floh	**alter**	(ver-, ab-)ändern
lane	Weg, Gasse, Pfad, Landstraße	**ladder**	Leiter
lain	gelegen (von: lie)	**letter**	Brief
wrap	einwickeln, einpacken	**pail**	Eimer, Kübel
rap	(an)klopfen (auf)	**pale**	blass, bleich, matt
flew	flog (von: fly)	**wrote**	schrieb (von: write)
flue	Rauchfang, Rauchabzug	**road**	Straße
flu	Grippe	**rode**	ritt, fuhr (von: ride)
ring	Ring, Kreis, läuten, klingeln	**drunk**	betrunken, getrunken (von: drink)
wring	winden, auswringen	**trunk**	Stamm, Koffer
claws	Pfoten, Krallen, packen, zerkratzen, reißen, greifen	**led**	geführt (von: lead)
		let	lassen
clause	Klausel, Vertragsbestimmung	**lead**	Blei(mine), Lot
won't	will nicht (von: will not)	**one**	ein(e, r, s), man
wont	Gewohnheit, Angewohnheit, gewohnt	**won**	gewonnen, gewann (von: win)
steel	Stahl	**been**	gewesen (von: be)
steal	stehlen	**bean**	Bohne
course	Gang, Lauf, Fahrt, Kursus	**pause**	Pause, Schweigen
coarse	rau, grob, gewöhnlich, roh	**paws**	Pfoten, (er) berührt
die	sterben, dahinscheiden	**scene**	Szene
dye	bleichen, färben, Farbstoff	**seen**	gesehen (von: see)
none	niemand, keiner	**bow**	Bogen, Verbeugung
nun	Nonne, Klosterschwester	**bough**	Ast, Zweig
raise	hochziehen, erheben	**foul**	unfair, unsportlich
rays	Strahlen	**fowl**	Geflügel
dew	Tau	**blade**	Klinge, Sägeblatt
due	zahlbar, fällig, gehörig	**plate**	Teller

toe	Zehe, Spitze	**sights**	Sehenswürdigkeiten
tow	abschleppen	**sites**	Grundstücke
tuck	Saum, sticken	**practice**	Übung, Gewohnheit
tug	ziehen, zerren, reißen	**practise**	(aus)üben, proben
wile	Trick, List	**wine**	Wein
while	während, zwar, Weile	**whine**	wimmern, Gejammer
brought	brachte (von: bring)	**dessert**	Nachtisch
broad	breit, hell	**desert**	Wüste
loose	lose, frei, locker	**week**	Woche
lose	verlieren, einbüßen	**weak**	schwach, lasch
price	Verkaufspreis, Wert	**cote**	Schutzdach, Stall
prize	Gewinn, Preis	**code**	Chiffre, Code
prise	aufbrechen	**coat**	Jacke, Mantel
jack	Wagenheber	**wood**	Wald
Jack	Hans	**would**	wollte (von: will)
rice	Reis	**safe**	Safe, Tresor, sicher
rise	aufstehen, sich erheben	**save**	sparen, retten
aunt	Tante	**vale**	Tal
ant	Ameise	**wail**	wimmern
aren't	sind nicht (von: are not)	**whale**	Wal
sun	Sonne	**main**	Haupt-...(-straße)
son	Sohn	**mane**	Mähne
of	von, aus (Besitz)	**litre**	Liter (Maß)
off	weg, ab, aus (Entfernung)	**litter**	Abfall, verstreuen
bag	Tasche, Beutel, Sack	**hare**	Hase
pack	(ein)packen	**heir**	Erbe
beg	bitten	**hair**	Haar
which	welche(r,s)	**weight**	Gewicht
witch	Hexe	**wait**	warte(n)
cent	Cent (amerik. Münze)	**born**	geboren, entstehen (Idee)
sent	schickte, geschickt (von: send)	**borne**	getragen, ertragen (von: bear)
send	senden, schicken		

Englische Redewendungen (Idioms)

Es macht sich immer gut, typische Redewendungen zu verwenden. Die folgende Auswahl hilft sicherlich dabei.

about here	ungefähr hier
all / just the same	trotzdem
behind the scenes	hinter den Kulissen
behind the times	rückständig sein
in cold blood	kaltblütig
it's blowing great guns	es stürmt
I am blown	ich bin sprachlos / platt
to break down	zusammenbrechen, kaputtgehen, aussetzen
to bring up a matter	etwas zur Sprache bringen
to bury the hatchet	das Kriegsbeil begraben
by and by	nach und nach, bald, nächstens
to call for	jmdn. abholen
to call off	absagen
to call up	anrufen
to call in question	in Frage stellen, bezweifeln
it's raining cats and dogs	es gießt in Strömen
to fish for compliments	sich Komplimente machen lassen
to return a compliment	sich revanchieren, etwas vergelten
his courage failed him	sein Mut verließ ihn
as pale as death	kreidebleich, totenbleich
he departed from his word	er hielt nicht Wort
to have done with s.th.	Schluss mit etwas machen
on the dot	pünktlich auf die Minute
to drop a person	jmdn. fallen lassen
to drop in	kurz besuchen
to be engaged to s.o.	verlobt sein
to give an eye to s.th.	ein Auge auf etwas haben
a black eye	ein „blaues Auge"
face to face	von Angesicht zu Angesicht
to finish in / on time	rechtzeitig fertig werden
a pretty kettle of fish	eine schöne Bescherung
to fire away	losschießen, sich beeilen, rennen
first or last	früher oder später
free and easy	ungezwungen
as gentle as a dove	sanft wie eine Taube
to get rid of s.o.	jmdn. loswerden
to give oneself away	sich verraten
to give way	nachgeben
it's high time to go	es ist höchste Zeit zu gehen
as old as the hills	uralt
to break the ice	das Eis brechen
the jig is up	da ist nichts mehr zu machen
just like ...	ganz wie ...

to kill time	die Zeit totschlagen
to lay the table	den Tisch decken
to make fun of	sich lustig machen über
to make one's luck	sein Glück machen
to make a pair	heiraten
to mean well	die besten Absichten haben
a month of Sundays	sehr selten, alle Jubeljahre
next door to	beinahe schon, nahezu
in the nick of time	im letzten Augenblick
to give a notice	kündigen
off-hand	aus dem Stegreif, ohne weiteres
once upon a time	es war einmal ...
in order	in Ordnung
over and over again	wiederholt
What a pity!	Wie schade!
to take place	stattfinden
out of place	unangebracht, unpassend
to play off	gegeneinander ausspielen
I am pleased with you	ich bin zufrieden mit dir
it's a poor argument	es ist eine schlechte Begründung
as poor as a church mouse	arm wie eine Kirchenmaus
a pretty job	eine saubere Sache
to pull a person's leg	jmdn. aufziehen
to pull oneself together	sich zusammennehmen
to pull strings	Beziehungen spielen lassen
to pull together	an einem Strick ziehen, zusammenhalten
to put off	verschieben, aufschieben
a burning question	eine brennende / dringende Frage
to be out of the question	nicht in Frage kommen
at any rate	auf jeden Fall
a red herring	ein Ablenkungsmanöver
as regular as clockwork	regelmäßig wie ein Uhrwerk
to ride high	erfolgreich sein
to be on the rocks	pleite sein
to get the sack	entlassen werden
to make no secret of s.th.	kein Geheimnis aus etwas machen
to see at a glance	erkennen, auf den ersten Blick sehen
to sell off	ausverkaufen
to settle down	sich niederlassen
like a shot	blitzschnell, wie aus der Pistole
on the spot	auf der Stelle
to take after s.o.	jmdm. nachschlagen / ähneln
to take off	starten
to talk over s.th.	etwas besprechen
a tall story	eine unglaubliche Geschichte
to have a good time	sich amüsieren
to be pressed for time	keine Zeit haben, in Zeitnot sein
to top up a glass	ein Glas bis zum Rand füllen
he is true in his word	er ist ehrlich, er hält sein Wort
to blow one's own trumpet	sich selbst loben

to try one's fortune	sein Glück versuchen
it's your turn	du bist dran / an der Reihe
to twinkle one's eyes	mit den Augen zwinkern, blinzeln
ups and downs	Höhen und Tiefen
to upset a person	jmdn. aus der Fassung bringen
he is used to it	er ist daran gewöhnt
very nearly	fast, um ein Haar
to have in view	im Auge haben, sich vornehmen
to speak volumes	Bände sprechen
to vote against / for	stimmen gegen / für
to walk one's bicycle	sein Fahrrad schieben
to be in deep water	in Not sein
by the way	übrigens
to weather the storm	die Lage meistern
I'm well	es geht mir gut
whether you like it or not	ob es dir passt oder nicht
to leave word	eine Nachricht hinterlassen

Englische Satzbaumuster

Der Englischunterricht schreibt die Strukturen verbindlich vor. Man sollte sie daher kennen und immer wieder in Sätzen anwenden. Hier ist eine wichtige Auswahl.

Jemanden begrüßen:

- Hello, Hi, Hallo, ...
- Good morning / afternoon / evening / night

Sich selbst oder jemanden vorstellen:

- I'm ... / My name is ...
- This is ... / John, this is ...

Fragen, wie Personen oder Dinge heißen, und darauf antworten:

- What's your / her / his name?
- Who's he / she / this?
- My / Her / His name's ...
- Are you ...? – Yes, I am. – No, I'm not.
- Is he / she ...? – Yes, he / she is ... – No, he / she isn't ...
- What's this in English? – It's a ...
- Is this a ... or ...?
- What's that? – It's ...

Fragen, wo sich jemand oder Dinge befinden, und darauf antworten:

- Where's / where are ...? – The ... is / are in / on / under / ...
- It's in / on / under / near / behind / ...
- Is the ... in / on / under ...? – Yes, it is. / No, it isn't.
- Is there a ... in / on / under ...? – Yes, there is. / No, there isn't.
- There's a ... in / on / under ...

Fragen, wem Dinge gehören, und darauf antworten:

- Whose ... is this / that? – It's Tom's.
- Is this my / your / etc. ...? – This is my / your / etc. ...
- Have you got a ...? – Has he / she got a ...?
- Yes, I have. / No, I haven't. / Yes, he / she has. / No, he / she hasn't.

Nach Mengen und Preisen fragen und Auskunft geben:

- How many ... are there in / on / under ... How many ... have you / has he / she got?
- I've got ... / He's / She's got ...
- How much is / are ...?
- It's ... / They're ...

Nach Uhrzeit und Datum fragen und Auskunft geben:

- What time is it? – It's ...
- What's the time, please? – It's ...
- When / what time does the train leave?
- It / The ... leaves – At / After / On ...
- What day is it today? – It's ...
- What's the date, please? – It's ... / Today is the third of June.
- When's your birthday? – It's on ...

Fragen, was Personen und Dinge können, und darauf antworten:

- Can you / he / she / ...? – Yes, he / she / ... can. / No, he / she / ... can't.
- I can ... / He can ... – I can't ... / He can't ...

Fragen, welche Eigenschaften (Größe, Farbe, Alter) Personen oder Dinge haben, und Auskunft geben:

- What colour is ...? – It's blue / ...
- Is your ... old / new / ...? – Yes, it's ... / No, it's ...
- It's a big / ...

Fragen, was Personen oder Tiere gerade tun, und darauf antworten:

- What's ... doing (just now)?
- He / She is ...ing. / I'm ...ing. / They are ...ing.

Fragen, was Personen oder Tiere gewohnheitsmäßig tun, und darauf antworten:

- What do you do on Sunday / ... evenings / ...?
- I watch TV. / He / She watches TV.
- When do you / does he / she / ...?
- I always ... after breakfast / ...

Nach Vorlieben und Abneigungen von Personen und Dingen fragen, und darauf antworten:

- Do you like ...? Does he / she like ...?
- Yes, I do. / No, I don't. / She doesn't.
- I like ... – I don't like ... – He / She doesn't like ...

Einen Wunsch oder eine Bitte äußern und darauf reagieren:

- Can I have ..., please?
- Go to / give me / bring me / get ..., please.
- Here it is. / Here you are.
- Clean the board, please. – Put the ..., please.
- Take this letter to ..., please.
- Don't ...
- All right.
- Sorry, I can't / haven't got ...

Nach dem Weg fragen und entsprechende Auskunft geben:

- Excuse me, where's ...?
- How can I get to ...?
- Go down ..., turn right / left at ..., cross ...

Sich bedanken und auf Dank reagieren:

- Thank you.
- Thank's.
- That's all right.
- You're welcome.

Jemanden begrüßen und sich verabschieden:

- Good morning / afternoon / evening.
- How are you? – Fine, thank you. And you?
- Goodbye.

Jemanden beglückwünschen und darauf antworten:

- Happy birthday, ...
- Merry Christmas and a Happy New Year, ...
- The same to you.

Nach Eigenschaften von Personen und Dingen fragen und entsprechend antworten:

- What does ... look like?
- How old is ... / are you?
- What's he like?

Nach Herkunft, Aufenthalt und Alter fragen und darauf antworten:

- What's your nationality?
- Where are you from?
- Are you from ...?
- Where do you live?
- What's your address?
- Where are you staying?
- How old are you?
- When were you born?
- When was ... born?

Fragen, was jemand in der Zukunft vorhat, und auf entsprechende Fragen antworten:

- What are you going to do next Saturday?
- We're going to make a cake.
- I'm not going to wear ... today.

Fragen, was sich zu einem bestimmten Zeitpunkt in der Vergangenheit ereignet hat, und auf entsprechende Fragen antworten:

- Did everything go all right?
- What did you see? – I didn't see anything.
- Where / how / when did it happen?

Um etwas bitten und darauf reagieren:

- Excuse me. Can you help me, please?
- Can / may I see / have your ...?
- Can I see them?
- No, I'm sorry you can't.
- Of course, you can.

Jemandem etwas verbieten und auf Verbote reagieren:

- Please, don't ...
- You can't ...
- O.K.
- All right.
- Sorry, I didn't know ...

Jemandem zustimmen oder widersprechen:

- Yes, it is. / Well, yes.
- O.K. / All right.
- You're right. / That's right. / I think that's wrong.
- That's a good idea.
- I don't think so.

Sich nach Verpflichtungen erkundigen und auf entsprechende Fragen antworten:

- Do I have to ...? / Have I got to ...?
- You have to ... / You've got to ...
- You don't have to ... / You haven't got to ...

Vermutungen anstellen:

- I think ...
- I don't think ...

Gefühle ausdrücken:

- I hope ...
- I'm worried / frightened / afraid ...
- I'm so sorry.
- What a pity / shame!
- That's funny.

Nach Gründen fragen:

– Why ...?

Sich entschuldigen oder rechtfertigen:

– Sorry, I didn't ..., because ...
– I'm sorry to / that ...
– Sorry, I've got to ... / Sorry, I have to ...
– That's all right.

Einen Vorschlag machen und darauf reagieren:

– Why don't we ...?
– Let's ...
– What about ...?
– I'd love to ..., (but ...)
– All right, but I must ...
–

Auf Warenangebote reagieren:

– That's very / too ...
– It fits quite well.
– That looks ...
– Well, I'll take ...

Um Auskunft bitten und einer solchen Bitte entsprechen:

– What does ... mean? – That means that ...
– When does ...?
– I'm looking for ...
– Excuse me, is this seat taken?
– Do you know ...?
– My German size is ...

Um einen Gefallen bitten und darauf reagieren:

– Please ...
– Who can ...?
– I'd like (to) ...
– Could you ...?
– I need ...

Stellung nehmen zu Tätigkeiten:

– I hate / love ... (Zeitwort mit der Endung -ing)
– I like / don't like ... (Zeitwort mit der Endung -ing)
– I prefer ... (Zeitwort mit der Endung -ing)
– It was / it'll be / it's nice to ...

Vergleiche anstellen:

- She / he is as ... as ...
- Which ... is ... (comparative)
- The ... is ... than ...
- Who is the tallest boy / girl in your class?

Über vergangene Ereignisse und Tätigkeiten berichten, die in der Gegenwart nachwirken:

- Have you ... (past participle)
- I've (just / already) ... (past participle)
- I haven't ... (past participle) yet.

Berichten, was jemand anderer sagt oder gesagt hat:

- He says that Jenny is ill.
- He said that Jenny was ill.
- He told us that Fred has had an accident.

Die Abhängigkeit zweier Handlungen voneinander zum Ausdruck bringen:

- I'll ... if ...

Etwas versprechen:

- I'll do it.
- I'll ... of course.
- I won't ...

Einen Brief beginnen und beenden:

- Dear ...,
- Thank you for ...
- Love, John.
- Yours sincerely, Ann.

Zugeben, dass man etwas nicht weiß oder versteht:

- Sorry, I don't know.
- Pardon?
- Sorry, I don't / didn't understand ...
- What did you say?

Sich rückversichern:

- Is that right?
- That's ..., isn't it?

Auskunft einholen und geben über Entfernung und Dauer:

- How far is it to ...?
- How long will it take to ...?
- How long are you going to stay ...?
- It's about ... from here.
- It'll take (you) about ... / It takes (you) ...

Indirekt nach Ort, Zeit oder Grund eines Ereignisses fragen:

- Could you tell me where / when / why ...?

Nach Problemen fragen und sie schildern:

- What's the problem? / What's wrong?
- I've got a problem.
- I don't know if / how to ...
- The ... isn't working.
- I think the ... is out of order.

Nach persönlichen Eindrücken fragen und darauf antworten:

- What's / was ... like?
- What do you think of ...?
- How did you like ...?
- Did you enjoy ...?
- Why did you like ...?
- Isn't it ...?
- I think / thought it was ...
- It's a pity / shame that ...

Ein Telefongespräch aufnehmen:

- This is ... speaking.
- Hello, is that ...?
- Can I speak to ...? / Can you put me through to ...?

Personen und Dinge durch ihre Tätigkeiten näher kennzeichnen:

- Is that the man who gave you the flowers?
- Jack has bought a car that can do 110 m.p.h. (oder: mph)

Etwas anbieten:

- Can I help you? / Can I show you ...?
- What can I do for you?
- We've got some ...?
- Anything else?
- What ... would you like? / Would you like ... or ...?
- Are you interested in ...?
- What are you looking for?

Unterschiede feststellen:

- What is the difference between ...?
- ... is the most interesting film I have ever seen.

Einen Rat geben:

- Mind the / your ...
- You'd better ...
- You should / shouldn't ...
- What about ... (-ing form)
- Either ... or ...
- Try to ...

Freude ausdrücken:

- I'm looking forward to ...
- I'm glad to ...

Beim Telefonieren sich zuhörbereit zeigen und nach näheren Angaben fragen:

- I beg your pardon?
- Would you say that again, please?
- Who's speaking?
- Where are you speaking from?
- What's your number?
- Can I phone you back?
- Can I take a message?

Jemand einen Entschluss mitteilen:

- I'm going to ...
- I'm planning to ...

Alternative Pläne vorstellen:

- I could either ... or ...

Einwände machen und abwägen:

- I (don't) think / believe that ...
- Maybe, but I think ...

Ein Urteil begründen:

- I've made up my mind to ... because ...
- I think it's better to ... because ...

Überzeugtheit zum Ausdruck bringen:

- I'm sure that ...

Gleichgültigkeit äußern:

- I don't mind (...)
- I don't care (...)
- It doesn't matter (...)

Enttäuschung und Unzufriedenheit äußern:

- It's a pity that ...
- I'm afraid it's ...
- It wasn't a good idea to ...

Eine Präferenz ausdrücken:

- I'd rather ...
- I prefer ...

Englische Grammatik

In diesem Kapitel werden die wichtigsten englischen Grammatikregeln zusammengefasst, die man für den Alltag braucht. Es ist nicht nur wichtig, die Grammatik zu kennen und zu beherrschen, sondern auch immer wieder in Satzzusammenhängen sinngemäß anzuwenden. Alle Regeln werden durch Beispiele erläutert. Zu wichtigen grammatischen Besonderheiten werden weitere Übungsmöglichkeiten gegeben.

I. Substantiv

Mehrzahlbildung (Plural)

Regel: **Normalerweise wird im Englischen in der Mehrzahl ein -s an die Einzahlform (Singular) angehängt.**

Beispiele: *ball – balls, thing – things, window – windows*
I've got two balls.
The windows are broken.

Regel: **Bei englischen Substantiven mit den Endungen -x, -z, -ss, -sh, -ch, -s wird ein -es angehängt.**

Beispiele: *box – boxes, bus – busses, dish – dishes, crash – crashes*
Wash the dishes, please.
These bus(s)es are going to London.

Regel: **Bei englischen Substantiven mit der Endung -y wird in der Mehrzahl (Plural) ein -ies.**

Beispiele: *body – bodies, lady – ladies, cry – cries, city – cities*
The ladies talk in the garden.
There are many old cities in England.

Regel: **Bei Substantiven mit der Endung -o wird im Plural ein -oes.**

Beispiele: *negro – negroes, tomato – tomatoes, potato – potatoes, buffalo – buffaloes*
I like tomatoes.
There are a lot of buffaloes in the National Park.
Achtung! Ausnahme: photo – photos

Regel: **Einige englische Substantive ändern ihren Vokal bzw. ihre Form.**

Beispiele: *man – men, woman – women, foot – feet, mouse – mice*
child – children, cactus – cacti, tooth – teeth
There are more men in China than women.
Susan likes white mice.

Regel: Einige Substantive, die auf *-f* oder *-fe* enden, erhalten in der Mehrzahl (Plural) die Endung *-ves*.

Beispiele: *wife – wives, housewife – housewives, half – halves, knife – knives, calf – calves, thief – thieves, life – lives, leaf – leaves*
Leaves are falling in autumn.
Many thieves are imprisoned.
This year we have many calves.

Substantive ohne Mehrzahlform

Beispiele: *homework, progress, advice, furniture, information, sheep, damage, knowledge, business, traffic, food, labour, success, progress, machinery, evidence, people, fish, merchantise, money*
I do my homework every day.
Can you give me some advice, please?
There are many sheep on the road.
The traffic is heavy.

Substantive ohne Einzahlform

Beispiele: *trousers, jeans, shorts, swimming trunks, pyjamas, scissors, glasses, tights, scales, lungs, braces, clothes, wages, thanks, contents, vegetables, arms, belongings, spectacles, compasses, gallows, parents, stairs, news, goods*
My sister Anne has got many tights.
I need new glasses.
An octopus has some arms.
I buy a new jeans.

Merke: *single parent, one-parent child, one-parent family, single-parent family, I as a single parent ...*

Die Besitzform

Sie zeigt, wem etwas gehört. Im Englischen gibt es dafür zwei Möglichkeiten: den *sächsischen Genitiv* oder die Umschreibung mit *of*.

Regel: Beim sächsischen Genitiv, der einen Besitz ausdrückt, wird bei Personen in der Einzahl an das Substantiv ein *'s* angehängt. In der Mehrzahl wird das Apostroph dann nach der Mehrzahlform angehängt.

Beispiele: *My father's hat is grey.*
The butchers' are closed today.
My sister´s room is clean.
St. Paul´s is in London.

Regel: Bei Gegenständen, Behältnissen, Mengenbezeichnungen und Maßen wird die Besitzform meist mit der Umschreibung *of* verwendet.

Beispiele: *a glass of wine, news of the day, the name of this city,*
one pound of tomatoes, an envelope of a letter
My father likes a glass of wine.
We need a pound of potatoes.

Wichtig! Im Englischen werden Hauptwörter kleingeschrieben, mit Ausnahme von Eigennamen.

Beispiele: *song, game, Trafalgar Square, German, Mr. Miller, Mrs. Fox*
Mrs. Keating goes to Oxford Circus in London to meet a German group.

II. Verb

Gegenwart

Regel: In der 3. Person Einzahl wird bis auf einige Ausnahmen (s. u.) an das Verb ein *-s* angehängt.

Beispiele: *laugh – she laughs, write – he writes, open – she opens, buy – he buys,*
lay – she lays, play – he plays, work – she works, keep – it keeps
Mike writes a letter.
My mother buys a new pair of shoes.

Regel: Bei Verben, die mit *-o* oder *-ch* enden, wird ein *-es* angehängt.

Beispiele: *I go – he goes, I do – she does, I watch – he watches, I catch – she catches*
I teach – she teaches
Jutta goes to the cinema.
Claudia does a good job.
Hans never watches TV.
Peter catches the train.
Mrs. Owen teaches in Reading now.

Regel: Bei Verben, die mit *-y* enden, wird aus dem *-y* ein *-ies*, wenn vor dem *-y* ein Mitlaut steht (beim Vokal bleibt das y).

Beispiele: *I hurry – he hurries, I bury – she buries, I fly – he flies, I cry – she cries*
Verena hurries to fetch the train.
The bird flies very high.
Aber: Mary stays at home.

Überblick:

Infinitiv (Grundform)				to sing	to do	to cry	to play	to teach
Singular	1. Pers.	I	(ich)	sing	do	cry	play	teach
	2. Pers.	you	(du)	sing	do	cry	play	teach
	3. Pers.	he	(er)	sings	does	cries	plays	teaches
		she	(sie)	sings	does	cries	plays	teaches
		it	(es)	sings	does	cries	plays	teaches
Plural	1. Pers.	we	(wir)	sing	do	cry	play	teach
	2. Pers.	you	(ihr)	sing	do	cry	play	teach
	3. Pers.	they	(sie)	sing	do	cry	play	teach

Die Vergangenheit

Regel: Im Englischen wird in der Vergangenheit normalerweise an die Grundform des Verbs ein *-ed* angehängt.

Beispiele: *open – opened, clear – cleared, talk – talked*
The passenger talked too much.
He listened to the music.

Regel: Bei Verben, die auf *-y* enden, wird in der Vergangenheit aus dem *-y* ein *-ie*, wenn vor dem *-y* ein Mitlaut steht.

Beispiele: *fly – flied, cry – cried, copy – copied, worry – worried*
Simon hurried to the cinema.
Mrs. Fox worried about her daughter.

Regel: Bei Verben, die auf *-e* enden, entfällt ein weiteres *-e*.

Beispiele: *invite – invited, agree – agreed, promise – promised, share – shared, care – cared, save – saved*
Winfried promised to learn more.
The teacher agreed.

Regel: Bei mehrsilbigen Verben, die auf *-l* enden, wird meist das *-l* verdoppelt.

Beispiele: *model – modelled, travel – travelled*
Carmen travelled to Glasgow last year.

Regel: Nach einem kurzen betonten Vokal werden die folgenden: Mitlaute verdoppelt *-b, -p, -t, -d, -g, -m, -s, -n*

Beispiele: *dig – digged, tip – tipped, admit – admitted*
Many men digged for gold in California many years ago.

Die Zukunft und Bedingung

Im Englischen gibt es mehrere Möglichkeiten, etwas Zukünftiges auszudrücken: mit *will* / *shall* und mit *going to.*

Regel: In der 1. Person Einzahl und Mehrzahl wird die Zukunft mit *shall* oder *will* gebildet, ansonsten immer mit *will.* Der Bedingungssatz wird in der 1. Person Einzahl und Mehrzahl mit *should* oder *would* gebildet, bei den übrigen Personen immer mit *would.*

Merke: In der Umgangssprache wird meist nur die Kurzform verwendet. Hinter *will* steht mehr Druck (dass man etwas wirklich tut oder machen will).

Überblick:

	Zukunft				Bedingung
I	shall/will	am	going to	play	should/would play
you	will	are	going to	play	would play
he/she/it	will	is	going to	play	would play
we	shall/will	are	going to	play	should/would play
you	will	are	going to	play	would play
they	will	are	going to	play	would play

Die Verlaufsform

Die Verlaufsform drückt eine Handlung aus, die entweder gerade abläuft, noch andauert oder noch nicht abgeschlossen ist, war oder sein wird.

Regel: Die Verlaufsform wird mit einer Form des Hilfszeitworts von *to be* gebildet. An das Zeitwort wird *-ing* angehängt.

Beispiele: *I am singing a nice song.*
It was raining yesterday.
I shall be working tomorrow.
Patrick was waiting for you.

Regel: Die Verlaufsform wird auch für geplante Handlungen verwendet. Dabei steht häufig eine Zeitangabe der Zukunft.

Beispiele: *I'm visiting the USA next summer.*
We are going to the disco next Saturday.
The train is leaving at 4 o'clock.

Regel: Wenn ein Zeitwort mit *-e* endet, entfällt das *-e.*

Beispiele: *write – writing, ride – riding, make – making*

Regel: Wenn englische Zeitwörter mit den Mitlauten *-t, -p, -l, -n* enden, werden diese verdoppelt.

Beispiele: *sit – sitting, stop – stopping, travel – travelling, begin – beginning, cut – cutting*

Regel: Wenn ein Zeitwort mit *-ie* endet, wird dieses zu *-y*.

Beispiel: *lie – lying, die – dying*
The ball is lying on the floor.

III. Hilfszeitwort

Überblick: Die Formen von *to be*

Personalform	Gegenwart to be		Vergangenheit		Perfekt	
I	am	(bin)	was	(war)	have been	(bin gewesen)
you	are	(bist)	were	(warst)	have been	(bist gewesen)
he/she/it	is	(ist)	was	(war)	has been	(ist gewesen)
we	are	(sind)	were	(waren)	have been	(sind gewesen)
you	are	(seid)	were	(wart)	have been	(seid gewesen)
they	are	(sind)	were	(waren)	have been	(sind gewesen)

Überblick: Die Formen von *to have*

Personalform	Gegenwart to have		Vergangenheit		Perfekt	
I	have	(habe)	had	(hatte)	have had	(habe gehabt)
you	have	(hast)	had	(hattest)	have had	(hast gehabt)
he/she/it	has	(hat)	had	(hatte)	has had	(hat gehabt)
we	have	(haben)	had	(hatten)	have had	(haben gehabt)
you	have	(habt)	had	(hattet)	have had	(habt gehabt)
they	have	(haben)	had	(hatten)	have had	(haben gehabt)

Überblick: Die Formen von *to do*

Personalform	Gegenwart to do		Vergangenheit		Perfekt	
I	do	(tue)	did	(tat)	have done	(habe getan)
you	do	(tust)	did	(tatest)	have done	(hast getan)
he/she/it	does	(tut)	did	(tat)	has done	(hat getan)
we	do	(tun)	did	(taten)	have done	(haben getan)
you	do	(tut)	did	(tatet)	have done	(habt getan)
they	do	(tun)	did	(taten)	have done	(haben getan)

Regel: Bei den folgenden Hilfszeitwörtern wird in der dritten Person Einzahl kein *-s* angehängt:

I you he/she/it we you they	must (müssen)	can (können)	will (wollen) (werden)	shall (sollen)	may (dürfen) (mögen)

Merke: Diese Kurzformen werden häufig gebraucht:

für: I am	I'm	für: you are	you're
für: he is	he's	für: it is	it's
für: she is	she's	für: we are	we're
für: they are	they're		
für: I have	I've	für: you have	you've
für: he has	he's	für: she has	she's
für: we have	we've	für: they have	they've
für: I will/shall	I'll	für: I would	I'd
für: are not	aren't	für: is not	isn't
für: do not	don't	für: does not	doesn't
für: has not	hasn't	für: have not	haven't
für: was not	wasn't	für: were not	weren't
für: had not	hadn't	für: cannot	can't
für: shall not	shan't	für: will not	won't
für: must not	mustn't	für: could not	couldn't
für: should not	shouldn't	für: did not	didn't

Beispiel: *I've been to Aberdeen.*
Susan wasn't at home.
Sorry, I can't give you my bike.
It's nice today, isn't it?

Merke: Die Hilfszeitwörter kommen besonders häufig bei Frage und Antwort vor (s. Abschnitt „Fragebildung").

IV. Eigenschaftswort (Adjektiv)

Es bestimmt ein Hauptwort oder Fürwort (Pronomen) genauer.

Beispiele: *a nice girl, an old car, a clean window, a difficult book*
This street is ugly.
My umbrella is old.
Susan is sad today.

Merke: Die Form des Eigenschaftswortes bleibt immer unverändert.
Die Steigerung mit -er und -est (regelmäßige Steigerung)

Regel: Einsilbige Eigenschaftswörter sowie zweisilbige Adjektive die auf *-y* enden, werden mit *-er* bzw. *-est* gesteigert (= regelmäßige Steigerung).

Merke: Ein -y am Ende wird dabei zu -i.

Beispiele: *old – older (than) – the oldest*
great – greater (than) – the greatest
happy – happier (than) – the happiest
lazy – lazier (than) – the laziest

Merke: **Bei Eigenschaftswörtern, die auf -e enden, entfällt bei dieser Steigerung ein -e.**

Beispiele: *fine – finer (than) – the finest*
Your cap is nice, but my cap ist nicer than yours.
The finest cap I've ever seen is in that shop.

Regel: **Wenn ein Eigenschaftswort auf -t, -n, -d, -g endet, werden diese Mitlaute verdoppelt, wenn vor ihnen ein kurz betonter Vokal steht.**

Beispiele: *big – bigger (than) – the biggest*

Regel: **Eigenschaftswörter mit zwei und mehr Silben werden mit *more* (mehr) und *most* (meist, am meisten) gesteigert.**

Beispiele: *difficult* *more diffcult (than)* *the most difficult*
boring *more boring (than)* *the most boring*
famous *more famous (than)* *the most famous*

Die unregelmäßige Steigerung

Manche Eigenschaftswörter werden unregelmäßig gesteigert.

Beispiele: *(gut)* *good* *better (than)* *the best*
(schlecht) *bad/ill* *worse (than)* *the worst*
(viel/viele) *much* *more (than)* *the most*
(wenig) *little* *less (than)* *the least*
It's good to learn for your exams.
It's better to do more for it.
To start today is best.

V. Umstandswort (Adverb)

Ein Umstandswort gibt eine weitere Information über ein Geschehen. Es bestimmt die Satzaussage genauer.

Regel: **Umstandswörter werden normalerweise gebildet, indem man an das Adjektiv ein *-ly* anhängt.**

Beispiele: *careful – carefully, slow – slowly, quick – quickly, dangerous – dangerously*
He runs very quickly.
She speaks slowly.
Mr. Miller drives dangerously.

Merke: **Ein Sonderfall ist *well*, das Umstandswort zu *good* (= gut).**

Beispiel: *He speaks English well.*

Regel: **Adjektive, die auf *-le* enden, verlieren diese letzte Silbe.**

Beispiele: *possible – possibly, noble – nobly, miserable – miserably*
He possibly goes to the USA to see Grand Canyon.
Robert plays the violin miserably.

Besondere Umstandswörter

Merke: **Bei einigen englischen Adjektiven wird kein *–ly* angehängt. Sie bleiben in der Normalform erhalten.**

Beispiele: *fast, early, long*
On the motorway some cars really go very fast.
I go up early in the morning.
He speaks very long.

VI. Fürwort (Pronomen)

Es gibt verschiedene Fürwörter: das persönliche Fürwort
das besitzanzeigende Fürwort
das rückbezügliche Fürwort
das hinweisende Fürwort
das unbestimmte Fürwort

Das persönliche Fürwort

Persönliche Fürworter ersetzen Hauptwörter oder Eigennamen und können als Satzgegenstand oder als Satzergänzung verwendet werden. Die Form ist unterschiedlich.

Überblick:

		Satzgegenstand		Satzaussage
Einzahl	I	ich	me	mir/mich
	you	du/Sie	you	dir/dich/Sie/Ihnen
	he	er	him	ihm/ihn
	she	sie	her	ihr/sie
	it	es	it	ihm/es
Mehrzahl	we	wir	us	uns
	you	ihr/Sie	you	euch/Ihnen/Sie
	they	sie	them	ihnen/sie

Beispiele: *He likes me.*
Have you got a bike?
I can't call them.

Merke: ***you* (= du, ihr, Sie) entspricht auch dem deutschen *man*.**

Beispiel: *You can go this way. Man kann diesen Weg gehen. Du kannst/Sie können diesen Weg gehen.*

Das besitzanzeigende Fürwort

Hierbei gibt es allein stehende Fürwörter, die als Hauptwort gebraucht werden und Fürwörter, die vor einem Substantiv stehen.

Überblick:

in Verbindung mit einem Hauptwort		allein stehend	
my book	mein	mine	meines, der/die/das meinige
your car	dein/Ihr	yours	deines/Ihres, der/die/das deinige/Ihrige
his bike	sein	his	seines, der/die/das seine
her umbrella	ihr	her	ihres, der/die/das ihrige
its food	sein		
our school	unser	ours	unseres, der/die/das unsrige
your machine	euer/Ihr	yours	eures/Ihres, der/die/das eurige/Ihrige
their van	ihr	theirs	ihres, der/die/das ihrige

Beispiele: *It's not my book. It's yours. Or is it ours?*
Yours is good but ours is best.
Sue has a nice dog. Its name is Roger.

Merke: **Wenn man bei Tieren das Geschlecht kennt, kann man auch die männliche (his) oder weibliche (her) Form verwenden.**

Beispiel: *He's a good watchdog.*

Das hinweisende Fürwort

Mit den hinweisenden Fürwörtern weist man auf etwas hin. Sie können alleine oder vor einem Substantiv stehen.

Singular		Plural	
this	dieser, diese, dieses	these	diese
that	jener, jene, jenes	those	jene

Beispiele: *This board is green and that blanket is brown.*
These sandals are nicer than those.

Merke: ***this / these* ist in der Nähe, bei *that/those* deutet man auf etwas, das weiter entfernt ist.**

Das rückbezügliche Fürwort

Das rückbezügliche Fürwort bezieht sich auf eine Person oder es betont, dass jemand etwas selbst getan hat oder gerade macht.

Regel: **In der Einzahl wird -*self* angehängt, in der Mehrzahl -*selves*.**

Beispiele: *I go to the teacher myself.*
Did they do it themselves?

Überblick:

Formen		Beispiele	
myself	mich	I enjoy myself	ich amüsiere mich
yourself	dich	you enjoy yourself	du amüsierst dich
himself	sich	he enjoys himself	er amüsiert sich
herself	sich	she enjoys herself	sie amüsiert sich
itself	sich	it enjoys itself	es amüsiert sich
ourselves	uns	we enjoy ourselves	wir amüsieren uns
yourselves	euch	you enjoy yourselves	ihr amüsiert euch
themselves	sich	they enjoy themselves	sie amüsieren sich

Das unbestimmte Fürwort some – any

some / something = etwas, (irgend-)ein – **Abkürzung:** *s.th.* oder auch *sth*
somebody / someone = (irgend-)jemand – **Abkürzung:** *s.o.* oder auch *so*

Regel: *some* **und seine Zusammensetzungen stehen**
– in bejahenden Sätzen und
– in Fragesätzen, wenn man eine bejahende Antwort erwartet.

Beispiele: *Would you like some marmalade? – Yes, please.*
Do you want some butter? – Yes, please.
I'd like something to drink, please.
Someone / Somebody has stolen my jacket.
If I had some money I would travel around the world.

any / anything = (irgend-)etwas, welche(r,s)
anybody / anyone = (irgend-)jemand, irgendeiner

Regel: *any* **und seine Zusammensetzungen stehen**
– in verneinten Sätzen,
– in Fragesätzen, deren Antwort ungewiss ist,
– in Fragesätzen, wenn man eine negative Antwort erwartet,
– in verneinten Bedingungssätzen.

Beispiele: *I haven't got any friends in New York.*
Is there anybody / anyone who speaks French?
Can I do anything for her?

Fragewort

Fragewort		Beispiele	
Who?	Wer?	Who are you?	– I'm Mike.
Whose?	Wessen?	Whose bike is it?	– John's.
Whom?/Who?	Wem?/Wen?	Whom did you give flowers?	– Susan.
What?	Was?	What's wrong with you?	– Nothing.
Which?	Welche(r, s)?	Which is the shortest way?	– That way.
Where?	Woher?	Where are you from?	– Germany.
Why?	Warum?	Why are you crying?	– Because ...
Where?	Wo?/Wohin?	Where are you going to?	– To ...
How much?	Wie viel?	How much is it?	– One pound.
How many?	Wie viele?	How many cats have you got?	– Many.
How long?	Wie lange?	How long will you play?	– Two hours.

VII. Bindewort (Konjunktion)

Bindewörter verbinden zwei Sätze miteinander. Hierbei gibt es mehrere Arten.

einräumend:	but	(aber)
	(al)though	(obwohl)
anreihend:	not only ... but also	(nicht nur ..., sondern auch ...)
	and	(und)
begründend:	because	(weil)
	as	(wie, weil)
zeitlich:	till	(bis)
	when	(als)
	after	(nach)
	as soon as	(sobald wie)
	before	(bevor)
	while	(während)

Beispiele: *Don't go to Mike before you have done your homework.*
I like milk but I don't like lemonade.
We don't go to this party because the last one was very boring.
But next time I'll bring my own music.
Susan is as nice as Angela.
You can play the trumpet while I am in the garden.
I go shopping after I have done my homework.
Travelling is not only nice but also interesting.
I lived in Munich when I was young.
Come as soon as possible.

VIII. Verhältniswort (Präposition)

Verhältniswörter zeigen Beziehungen zwischen verschiedenen Gegenständen oder Personen an. Dabei gibt es mehrere Möglichkeiten:

Lagebezeichnungen:

in, inside	(in, innen)	**outside**	(außen, außerhalb)
at	(an, am)	**on**	(auf, oben)
under	(unter)	**beside**	(neben)
behind	(hinten, hinter)	**in front of**	(vor, vorne, davor)
over	(über)	**out**	(hinaus)
round	(um ... herum, um)	**between**	(zwischen)
here	(hier)	**near, next to**	(in der Nähe, bei, nahe)
above	(oben)		

Richtungsbezeichnungen:

after	(nach, hinterher)	**into**	(hinein)
across	(über, drüben, quer)	**to**	(nach)
round	(um ... herum, um)	**against**	(gegen, an)
onto	(auf, hinauf)	**up**	(hinauf)
through	(durch)	**from**	(von)
down	(hinunter)	**off**	(herunter)
out of	(hinaus)	**over**	(über, darüber)
along	(entlang)	**away**	(weg)

Zeitbezeichnungen:

ago	(vor)	**about**	(gegen, ungefähr, etwa)
since	(seit – Zeitpunkt)	**in**	(in)
by	(bis zum ..., gegen)	**on**	(am)
from ... to	(von ... bis)	**for**	(seit – Zeitdauer)
at	(etwa, um – Uhrzeit)		

IX. Die Fragebildung

Regel: Im Englischen können Fragesätze mit einem Fragewort oder mit einem Hilfszeitwort beginnen.

Beispiele: *Who is your favourite popstar?*
Do you speak English? – Yes, of course.

Regel: **Wenn man eine Frage mit *Ja* oder *Nein* beantworten kann (sog. Entscheidungsfragen), beginnt der Satz mit einer der Formen von *to be* *(am, is, are, was, were)*, *to have* *(has, had)*, *can (could)*, *will (would)*, *may (might)*, *shall (should)* oder *must*.**

Frage	Antwort
Are you clever?	Yes, of course.
Is Mike in France?	No, he isn't. He is in Norway.
Are they at home?	No, they aren't. They are abroad.
Was John in the USA?	Yes, he was. He saw Grand Canyon.
Were they in China?	No, it was too expensive.
Have you got a bike?	Yes, I've got a bike.
Can he play the piano?	Yes, he plays it very well.
Could you help me, please?	Yes, of course.
Must we do that?	No, you mustn't.
Will you sing a song?	Not now, but later.
Would you do that for me?	Yes, certainly.
May I help you?	Thank you.

Regel: **Wenn kein Hilfszeitwort im Satz ist, bildet man die Frage mit einer Form des Hilfszeitwortes von *to do (does, did)*.**

Beispiele: *Do you like this music? – Yes, it's fantastic.*
Did you go to the cinema yesterday? – No, we didn't.

X. Der Satz

Satzarten

Wichtig sind folgende Satzarten:
– Aussagesatz
– verneinter Satz
– Fragesatz
– Relativsatz

Beispiele: Aussagesatz: *Bianca writes a letter.*
verneinter Satz: *Tom doesn't do his homework.*
Fragesatz: *Does Bill go to the cinema next Friday?*
Relativsatz: *The cat that cried was our neigbour's.*

Bei diesen Satzarten sollte man Satzteile und Wortstellung kennen.

Die Satzteile

Die Grundstellung ist: Satzgegenstand   – Satzaussage   – Satzergänzung
                        Subjekt   – Prädikat   – Objekt(e)

Beispiele: *My mother*   *works*   *in the garden.*
             The cat   *catches*   *a mouse.*
             Tom and Susan   *dance*   *in the disco.*

Merke: **Die Zeitangabe steht normalerweise am Ende, es sei denn, sie ist
             besonders betont oder sehr wichtig, dann kann sie auch am Satzanfang
             stehen.**

Beispiele: *My mother works in the kitchen every day.*
             Every Friday I go to the disco to meet my friends.
             (gemeint ist: nur **jeden** Freitag)

Regel: **Zeitangaben wie *often, sometimes, usually, never* stehen *vor*
             dem Verb.**

Beispiele: *I never go to the cinema. – He usually goes to Italy. – I often play football. –
             She sometimes plays the guitar.*

Die Leideform (Passiv)

Die Leideform sagt etwas über eine Handlung aus.

Gegenüberstellung: Aktiv – Passiv

Aktiv	Passiv
Oliver sings a song.	A song is sung by Oliver.
In Bavaria they make good beer.	Good beer is made in Bavaria.
People play tennis everywhere.	Tennis is played everywhere.
They speak French here.	French is spoken here.
Mary gives Peter a present.	A present was given to Peter.
They open a new firm in ...	A new firm was opened in ...
Bob broke a window.	A window was broken by Bob.
The cat caught a mouse.	A mouse was caught by the cat.

Wichtig!   **Denken Sie daran, dass bei den unregelmäßigen Verben im Passiv die
               dritte Form des Verbs in Verbindung mit einer Form von *to be* verwendet
               wird.**

Relativsatz

Er erläutert einen Hauptsatz in einem Nebensatz näher.

Wichtig ist die folgende Regel:

Regel: who/whom/whose/of whom bei Personen
that   bei Dingen und Tieren

Beispiele: *My friend John*   *always helps me.*
            (Nebensatz:)   *who is a nice boy*

            The dog   *is not here today.*
            (Nebensatz:)   *that bit me yesterday*

Bedingungssatz

Er besteht aus zwei Teilen: einem Haupt- und einem Nebensatz.
Der Nebensatz beginnt mit **if** (if = wenn, falls)

Beispiele: *If I had money I would travel around the world. – We do our homework first if it rains. –*
            If you want to go to Hamburg you must go by train.

Direkte und indirekte Rede

Sie wird verwendet, wenn man über etwas berichtet, was ein anderer gesagt hat. Die Gegenüberstellung zeigt dir den Unterschied:

wörtliche Rede	indirekte Rede
Lisa says, "*I go to the cinema.*"	Lisa said (that) she went to the cinema.
"*I am the* best," he shouts.	He shouted he was the best.
"*She is a nice girl.*"	... she was nice girl.
Hans says, "*I don't understand what you say.*"	Hans said he didn't understand what you said.

Das Komma

Regel: Das Komma steht

- **vor der direkten Rede,**
  (*He said, "I go to London."*)
- **im Brief nach der Überschrift und der Schlussformel,**
  (*Dear Mike, ... – Yours, Susan*)
- **beim Datum vor der Jahreszahl,**
  (*June 6th, 2015*)
- **vor und nach Adverbien**
  (*on the contrary, on the other hand, too, for example, anyhow, moreover, indeed, however*)
- **bei Tausendern wegen der besseren Übersichtlichkeit,**
  (14,512 für vierzehntausendfünfhundertundzwölf)
- **vor dem reflexiven Fürwort (Relativpronomen) "which".**
  (*The soldiers began to shoot, which was the beginning of a revolution*)

Wichtig: Das Komma wird nicht vor notwendigen Relativsätzen (z. B. vor "that" oder "who", "which") gesetzt. Es steht jedoch vor sog. ausmalenden Relativsätzen.

Beispiele: Lincoln was the president who was shot.
The ship that sank was too old.
Peter, who really is a nice boy, still goes to school.

Silbentrennung

Sie ist im Englischen sehr kompliziert. Es gibt viele Ausnahmen. Wir geben daher den Tipp, kein englisches Wort zu trennen.

Regel: Nicht getrennt werden:
- einsilbig gesprochene Wörter
- Wörter, bei denen ein einzelner Vokal auf einer Zeile stehen müsste

Regel: Getrennt wird nach Wortbestandteilen (Vorsilben, Endungen, Mitlauten, die beim Anhängen der Endung verdoppelt werden) und bei zwei Vokalen.

Übungsteil zu ausgewählten Bereichen

Dieser Übungsteil ist als Vertiefung und Ergänzung gedacht, um den Grundwortschatz, die Grammatik usw. im vorderen Teil zu vertiefen und anzuwenden, um die Sprachkompetenz zu verbessern.

Übung 1: Monate

Personen und die entsprechenden Monate einsetzen

Beispiel: *My uncles birthday is in ...*
usw. –

Übung 2: Länder – Sprachen – Volksgruppen

* Ordnen Sie den folgenden Ländern / Staaten Sprache und Nationalität zu. Bei einigen Ländern gibt es mehrere Möglichkeiten.

Canada – Belgium – France – Great Britain – Holland – Greece –America – Ireland – China – Germany – Switzerland – Turkey – England – Portugal –Spain – Bavaria – Sweden – Scotland – Denmark – Russia – Norway – Mexico – Hungary – Wales – Italy – Japan – Australia – Egypt – Austria – Namibia – Morocco – Greenland – Texas – Hongkong

British – American – English – Canadian – Texan – French – Greek – Danish – Bavarian – American – Irish(man) – Gaelic – Spanish – Welsh – German – Chinese – Russian – Dutch – Italian – Turk(ish) – Norwegian – Portuguese – Scotswoman/Scotsman – Flemish – Scot(tish) – Swiss – Hungarian – Namibian – Japanese – Moroccan – Swedish – Austrian – Egyptian – Mexican – Australian – Arabic – Belgian

Übung Sätze bilden:

Beispiel: *In Italy they / people speak Italian.*

* Setzen Sie jetzt dazu noch die Volksgruppe dazu:

Beispiel: *In America Americans speak ...*

British, Texan, Bavarian, American, Irish(man), Gaelic Welsh, German, Namibian, Swiss, Scotswoman / Scotsman, Moroccan, Austrian, Egyptian, Australian, Belgian, Mexican, ...

Übung 3: Gegenwörter (Opposites)

* Formulieren Sie Sätze zu den Gegenwörtern im vorderen Teil (S. 37 / 38)

Beispiel: *The opposite of ... is ...*

Übung 4:

• Was ist das Gegenteil zu den folgenden Wörtern?

dead...	uncertain...	love...	top...
ask...	send...	rich...	full...
forget...	ugly...	behind...	beautiful...
quiet...	wife...	low...	always...
weak...	important...	late...	powerful...
day...	with...	poor...	progressive...
gentleman...	clean...	quickly...	nice...
sister...	sunny...	easy...	death...
many...	good...	interesting...	true...
open...	city...	centre...	in...
here...	arrival...	start...	work...
buy...	see...	courage...	dark...
import...	agree...	dangerous...	waiter...
war...	slowly...	healthy...	hard...

• Finden Sie zunächst selbst Möglichkeiten. Weitere sind im Kasten versteckt. Ein Tipp: Wenn man die richtigen Wörter umrahmt, fällt die Zuordnung leichter.

```
hfgholidayirdmenhegpoordzquicklytrgdznicetrgfhhffegdzdisagreefgrdhegdzsafetrgfhhgdz
harmlessfgrdhzpeacetrgfhkffegdzlandtrgfhhffegdzsellfgrdhegdzlighttrgfhhffegdzbreakfgrh
egdzdeparturetrgfhhffegdzdirtytrdzconservativefgrdzillfgrdhzwithouttrgfhhffegdzrichtrgfha
ffegdznightfgrdhegdzearlyfgrdhegdizstrongtrwomengfhdznevertrgflasthhffegdzexportfgrrt
hightrgfhhffegdznoisyfgrdhegdzinfrontoffgrdhegdzanswertrgfhsadhgdzhatetrggdzalivefgzt
certainfgrdhegdzbottomtrgfdzgetfgzemptytrgfhhffdzpowerlesstrgegdzoutfgrdhegdzsuburt
fgrdhegdzfeartrgfhhffegdztherefgrdhegdzoutsidetrgfhhffegdzuntruefgrfunnydhegdzlifetrfh
workinghffegdzrainytrgfgrandmotherhhfbrotherfgrdhegdzrememberfgrdhegdzbadtrgegdh
somefgrdgdzdifficulttrfegdzuninterestingtrgfhhffegdzclosedfgrdhegdzvillagetrgfhhffdwarfa
gdzignoretrhfgdzbadfgrddayhegrandfathergdmanzslowlytrgdzsofttfgzunclefgrzaunttrgfhkn
hfsontrgfhhfirstegdzdaughterfgrdhegdzladytrgfhhffegdzgentlemantrgfhhffegdzleavefgrdee
hegdzblacktrgfhhffegdzwhitefgruiolfdhegdzhusbandfgrdgdzmothertrggdzfatherfgrdhegdzv
waitresjiopestrghndienwomanhölkheffegdzstewardfgrdhegdzstewardessöaknneönönpmlkj
```

• Einige Wörter und ihr Gegenteil bleiben übrig.

Übung 5: Oberbegriffe bilden

What is it?

- Ein Wort passt nicht in die Reihe. Was ist der Oberbegriff?

  Kopieren und vergrößern Sie diese Seite auf ein DIN-A4-Blatt und schreiben Sie den richtigen Oberbegriff daneben.

January – March – Monday – October – September   _____

carpet – chair – table – sofa – door   _____

Paris – Cologne – France – Munich – London   _____

quiet – nine – thirty-four – one hundred   _____

brother – sister – mother – friend – father   _____

copper – wood – iron – gold – silver   _____

chicken – goose – duck – tree   _____

breakfast – bread – supper – lunch   _____

apple – banana – clothes – pear   _____

Patrick – Oliver – Eric – Susan   _____

knife – screwdriver – car – hammer   _____

onion – cucumber – tree – tomato   _____

jacket – coat – cool – pullover   _____

summer – holiday – spring – winter – autumn   _____

Damit die Lösung nicht zu leicht fällt, ist sie hier versteckt. Ein Oberbegriff bleibt übrig.

---

hzefdte*vegetables*öourezc*clothes*süuzttrt*animals*pütz*metal*öiutexlt*meals*pütz*fruit*öpoiuzknm

bpoiukt*family*pztiuuftgdüz*boys*ötrrexhh*seasons*ktnumberspztownsölkjernölkjölkjztnfnönelk

ölkje*cities*loiurnwizilt*furniture*tzutüttuuuknneitölkejrlk*months*öiuznbtkenüennaq*tools*kihmom

- Jetzt geht es umgedreht. Nennen Sie zu den Oberbegriffen Beispiele. Unten geben wir Möglichkeiten durcheinander vor.

Kopieren und vergrößern Sie diese Seite auf ein DIN-A4-Blatt und schreiben Sie den richtigen Oberbegriff daneben.

relatives: _____

vegetables: _____

animals: _____

metal: _____

meals: _____

vehicles: _____

fruit: _____

family: _____

days: _____

boys (names): _____

numbers: _____

girls (names): _____

towns: _____

months: _____

furniture: _____

tools: _____

clothes: _____

- Ordnen Sie die Wörter zu:

table, forty, Monday, cookaburra, Eric, high tea, San Francisco, steak, coat, aluminium, lorry, aunt, February, lemon, chicken, tomato, pear, dog, Frank, train, thirty, nail, son, apple, tin, salad, Tuesday, Steve, daughter, breakfast, Peter, copper, lunch, grandfather, London, four, sheep, meat, May, father, January, cat, skirt, wire, Richard, Wednesday, strawberry, gold, five, bike, van, Edinburgh, wolf, Thursday, socks, Valerie, pliers, iron, cucumber, car, cupboard, bear, Sunday, Ingrid, shirt, tractor, New York, banana, supper, mother, uncle, Cardiff, lead, Susan, egg, twelve, screw, bird, sofa, Saturday, steel, silver, Hildegard, March, one, dinner, grandmother, eleven, bed, October, bicycle, pullover, chair, Patricia, bus, knife, orange, baby, Mike, fifty, Los Angeles, twice, stockings, hammer, two fifths, chair, December, screw-driver, Friday

Übung 6: Oberbegriffe

Was gehört zusammen?

Kopieren und vergrößern Sie diese Seite auf ein DIN-A4-Blatt und schreiben Sie den richtigen Oberbegriff daneben.

- Schreiben Sie die Wörter, die zusammengehören, nebeneinander. Manchmal ist es schwierig und verlangt Konzentration. Schauen Sie unbekannte Wörter nach. Wir geben die Bereiche vor.

shorts – new – grey – milk – potato – mountain – church – freeway – apple – heavy –

green – banana – historic – nice – silver – beer – ship – north – minor – flat – freighter –

pad – hill – tanker – mouse – unimproved – car – east – old – peach – hillock – boat – shirt

– lorry – lane –blue – ferry – oldish – latest – trawler – attracitve – beautiful – light – dou-

ble-decker – golden – serious – school – south – mouse – truck – alpes – ancient – hard –

van – cargo ship – west – coach – classical – easy – pear – charming – house – fresh –

beans – difficult – street – slight – red – skirt – oppressive – stale – wine – road – villa –

path –yellow – pig – cauliflower – second-hand – tomato – black – cow – motorway – wa-

ter – skyscraper – dog

Himmelsrichtungen: _____

Schiffe: _____

Fahrzeuge: _____

Berge: _____

schön: _____

neu: _____

schwierig: _____

einfach: _____

Verkehrswege: _____

alt: _____

Gebäude: _____

Kleidung: _____

Getränke: _____

Tiere: _____

Obst: _____

Gemüse: _____

Farben: _____

Übung 7: Amerikanisch – Englisch

Ein Amerikaner und Engländer unterhalten sich. Der Einfachheit halber wird der Dialog in Deutsch geschrieben. Schreiben Sie für das kursiv geschriebene Wort das amerikanische und das englische Wort.

Amerikaner: *Engländer:*

_____	*Hallo*, wie geht es Ihnen?	_____
_____	Ich komme gerade von der *Autobahn*.	_____
_____	Ich bin mit der *Eisenbahn* gefahren.	_____
_____	Ich muss erst einmal *Benzin* tanken.	_____
_____	Was ist Ihr *Familienname*?	_____
_____	Wo geht es zum *Universitätsgelände*?	_____
_____	Wie viel *Kinder* haben Sie?	_____
_____	Bald fahren wir in *Urlaub*.	_____
_____	Wo kann ich mein *Gepäck* einchecken?	_____
_____	Ich habe um 14 Uhr einen *Termin*.	_____
_____	Morgen bekomme ich den *Führerschein*.	_____
_____	Peter mag am liebsten *Fischstäbchen*.	_____
_____	Kannst du das Fahrrad *reparieren*?	_____
_____	Am liebsten mag ich *Erdbeergeschmack*.	_____
_____	Das Schiff erreicht den *Hafen* rechtzeitig.	_____
_____	Das Büro ist in der *1. Etage*.	_____
_____	Meine Stiefel sind im *Kofferraum*.	_____
_____	Weißt du die Postleitzahl?	_____
_____	Eine *einfache Fahrkarte*, bitte.	_____
_____	Gleich kommt die *U-Bahn*.	_____
_____	Hast du einen *Badeanzug*?	_____
_____	Ich esse am liebsten *Kartoffelchips*.	

88

Übung 8: unregelmäßige Verben

- Bei dieser Übung werden unregelmäßige Verben im Sinnzusammenhang angewandt. Bei den folgenden Sätzen kommen die regelmäßigen Formen der Vergangenheit ebenfalls vor. Die Grundform des Zeitworts bzw. Hilfzeitworts steht in der Klammer.

Kopieren und vergrößern Sie diese Seite auf ein DIN-A4-Blatt und schreiben Sie die richtige Vergangenheitsform daneben. Einige Sätze sind englische Redewendungen.

In a disco the music (be) _____ very loud. The sportswoman (fight) _____ for a cup. My father (play) _____ golf. A plane (flight) _____ to New York. Susan and Patrick (drink) _____ a Coke. A ball (hit) _____ me. My parents (thank) _____ God. I (know) _____ you (be) _____ in a hurry, but remember I (have) _____ to do my work. The burglers (hide) _____ themselves. Eric (play) _____ the piano very well. Mary (feed) _____ her horses. The clerk (sell) _____ a lot of things. Hildegard and Patrick (spend) _____ their holidays in Scotland. The bell (ring) _____ . The children (spell) _____ difficult words. The teacher (teach) _____ students every day. The helicopter (fly) _____ to Bonn. I (dream) _____ a dream every night but some people say they never had (dream) _____ one. I (keep) _____ my fingers crossed for your Quali. He (be) _____ good in football. They (keep) _____ the prices high. Frank always (meet) _____ a dead-line. Sue once (like) _____ riding a horse. The sailor (set) _____ sail. In the shop I (must) _____ empty the bag. The teacher (put) _____ two fighters apart. The king (wear) _____ a crown. Yesterday I (watch) _____ television at home. My friend (swim) _____ in a deep water. The composer (write) _____ some nice music. I (wrap) (!) _____ the rope round the tree. Henry (be) _____ as poor as a church mouse. It (mean) _____ a great deal to me. I (let) _____ him alone. My friend (lend) _____ me some money. The president (leave) _____ Berlin for London. I (help) _____ him to his feet. He (wish) _____ me good luck. I (love) _____ Katja. Some millionaires (begin) _____ as a diswasher. He (forget) _____ to blow the candles out. "Your ankle is (break) _____ , said the doctor to the football-player yesterday. "What (do) _____ you (eat) _____ ?" mother (ask) _____ . Smoking should be (forbid) _____ in schools and hospitals. The car was (drive) _____ by a man. The water was (freeze) _____ . Faults should be (forgive) _____ .

Übung 9: Homophones

• Zeigen Sie jetzt, ob Sie diese Wörter in Sätzen anwenden können. Kopieren und vergrößern Sie diese Seite auf ein DIN-A4-Blatt. Streichen Sie das falsche Wort durch und schreiben Sie das richtige Wort daneben.

My (deer / dear) _____ friend, I (hurt / heard) _____ that you (maid / made) _____ a nice (plane / plain) _____ in your freetime. Is it (red / read) _____ or green? I (no / know) _____ you like nice colours. Next Monday (eye / I) _____ am going to (meat / meet) _____ Mr Miller's (sun / son) _____ (inn / in) _____ an old (inn / in) _____ near Munich. Please send me (some / sum) _____ pictures (off / of) _____ your (knew / new) _____ (plane / plain) _____ . In your last letter you (road / rode / wrote) _____ me that your (farther / father) _____ planted a nice (fur / fir) _____ in your garden. (Buy / By / Bye) _____ the way (eye / I) _____ (past / passed) _____ my test last (week / weak) _____ . So (eye / I) _____ can go to the (sea / see) _____ on Saturday or (eye / I) _____ 'll stay at home and visit the (fair / fare) _____ in Munich, if it doesn't (reign / rain) _____ . Perhaps (eye / I) _____ 'll see my (ant / aunt) _____ there. She is a (none / nun) _____ . Did you lose some (wait / weight) _____ ? Oh, a big plane (flu / flue / flew) _____ above our house. (Were / Where) _____ have you been on Friday? (Eye / I) _____ was (in / inn) _____ the disco last (week / weak) _____ . It was nice. A man (blue / blew) _____ the trumpet. My mother just came from the (cote / code / coat) _____ . She fed the animals. (Eye / I) _____ 've got a nice young (hair / heir / hare) _____ . Our last one (dyed / died) _____ . My (farther / father) _____ was ill. So my mother called the dog / doc / dock) _____ . (Buy / Bye / By) _____ the way, my sister Sue (one / won) _____ a nice (prize / price / prise) _____ . It was a lovely (red / read) _____ (clog / clock) _____ . I must end now and (bag / pack / back) _____ my suitcase. Good (knight / night) _____ . Please (rite / write / right / ride) _____ me soon. Love, Mike

Übung 10: Wörter, die leicht verwechselt werden

- Die folgenden Wörter können von der Aussprache her leicht verwechselt werden. Daher ist es wichtig, den deutschen Begriff zu kennen.

food	→ foot	hat	→ hate	head	→ had	pig	→ big
quite	→ quiet	love	→ laugh	think	→ thing	beat	→ bead
path	→ bath	bark	→ park	pet	→ bed	to	→ do
time	→ dime	ton	→ done	boat	→ bought	plate	→ blade
planes	→ plans	few	→ view	build	→ built	pay	→ bay
bad	→ bat	there	→ their				

Übungsdiktat: Lasssen Sie sich von jemandem die folgenden Sätze diktieren. Hier kann man zeigen, ob man die leicht verwechselbaren Wörter auch schreiben kann. Die Wörter, auf die es hauptsächlich ankommt, wurden kursiv gedruckt.

In Hyde *Park there* are many dogs that might *bark*.

I *think there* are many *things* to *think* about.

The Foxes *build* a house now, but the Keatings *built* it last year.

Susan and Peter *love* each other. Don't *laugh* about *their love*.

Mr Barton *bought* a new car and a *boat*, too. He has *got* much money.

"Be *quiet*," *our* teacher said to a *quite* noisy class.

Dogs must have good *food*, and a *pig* likes *big* portions, too.

There are a *few* places in our village where I have a nice *view*.

I *hate* deep flying *planes*, because they are so noisy.

All people want to have *peace* in the world.

Please give me that *piece* of cake, I prefer it.

In London *there* are many *sites*, and tourists visit the *sights*, too.

My *aunt* Mary doesn't like *ants*, but she likes *dogs*.

I don't *know whether* there will be sunny *weather* tomorrow.

Pat *wrote* a letter, Susan played on the *road* and I *rode* on a horse.

I must learn a long *rhyme* till Thursday.

The tiny *flea flees* when people try to catch it.

Roy, our *male dog*, goes to the *docks* with me.

I still need a lot of *practice* to cycle well.

For dinner we had soup, fish and chips and a nice *dessert*.

Some *men* got *drunk* at the summer party. They drank *too* much *wine*.

"It's best to *save* your money in a bank *safe*," Peter said.

I *would* like to go to the *wood* to get some fresh air.

One hour ago *there* was a heavy *rain*.

Two hours ago it *rained* here, *too*.

The more you *practise* the better you are.

In America *there* live many *rich* people.

In *our* garden *there* are many big *firs*.

My father was *born* in Chicago, and my mother in Los Angeles.

We live in *Main* Street. In *which* street do you live?

Übung 11: Übungen zu den Satzbaumustern

Was würde man in folgenden Situationen sagen? Die Satzbaumuster im vorderen Teil helfen.

- Guten Morgen, Herr Miller, wie geht es Ihnen? – Sehr gut, danke.
- Wie viel Uhr ist es, bitte? – Es ist drei viertel sieben.
- Wie haben Sie geschlafen? – Sehr gut, danke.
- Herzlichen Glückwunsch zum Geburtstag. – Danke, vielen Dank.
- Wo ist Ihre Ehefrau? – Sie schläft noch.
- Ist sie krank? – Ich glaube, sie hat Magenschmerzen.
- Oh, wie schade, das wusste ich nicht.
- Was hat sie gestern gegessen? – Zu viel.
- Das stimmt, das ist nicht gut. – Natürlich.
- Es ist besser, nicht so viel zu essen. – Sie haben Recht.
- Ich hoffe, sie wird bald gesund. – Ich hoffe es auch.
- Was machen Sie morgen? – Ich wollte nach London fahren.
- Also, alles Gute und gute Besserung für Ihre Frau. – Danke.
- Hallo Walter! Wie geht es dir? – Mir geht es nicht so gut.
- Warum? – Ich habe meine Tasche verloren.
- Welche Farbe hat sie denn? – Sie ist gelb.
- Ist es eine neue Tasche? – Ja.
- Wo hast du sie denn verloren? – Ich glaube im Schwimmbad.
- Dann gehen wir doch einmal dorthin und fragen nach, oder?
- Das ist eine sehr gute Idee. – Kommst du mit?
- Natürlich werde ich dich begleiten. – Ich hole mein Fahrrad.

- Ich auch. – Treffen wir uns um 14 Uhr?
- Okay. Das ist eine gute Zeit. – Also bis 14 Uhr.
- Bis später. – Bis bald.
- Hallo! Wer bist du denn? – Ich heiße Eve und komme aus Reading.
  Entschuldigung, ich habe das nicht verstanden, woher kommst du?
- Ich komme aus Reading. – Wo ist denn das?
- Reading liegt westlich von London. – Wohnst du dort? – Ja.
- Dann bist du also Engländerin? – Ja.
- Wie alt bist du? – Ich bin fast sechzehn. Und wie alt bist du?
- Ich bin schon sechzehn. Wo wohnst du? Wie heißt deine Adresse?
- Ich wohne in der Hauptstraße 25 bei Familie Huber.
- Können wir uns heute Abend treffen? – Vielleicht, ich muss fragen.

• Was sagt man in folgenden Situtionen?

- Du erzählst einem Freund, was du werden möchtest.
- Man fragt dich, ob du Kaffee oder Tee möchtest. Antworte, dass es dir egal ist.
- Du wirst angerufen, hast aber im Moment keine Zeit. Frage, ob du zurückrufen kannst.
- Dein Freund ist traurig. Du fragst nach seinem Problem.
- Du entschuldigst dich bei deiner Freundin, dass du zu spät gekommen bist.
- Du fragst die Verkäuferin, ob du den Pullover anprobieren kannst.
- Rate deinem Freund mit dem Rauchen aufzuhören.
- Frage, was der Unterschied zwischen deutschem und amerikanischem Fußball ist.
- Sage, dass du planst im nächsten Jahr nach Schottland zu fahren.
- Sage, dass du mit dem Zug oder mit dem Bus fahren könntest.
- Sage, dass du dich entschlossen hast, mit dem Zug zu fahren.
- Du glaubst, dass es in Schottland fast jeden Tag regnet.
- Sage, dass du dich auf deine Geburtstagsparty am Donnerstag freust.
- Du befürchtest, dass Michael nicht kommen kann.
- Du glaubst, dass es keine gute Idee ist, im Garten zu tanzen.
- Du hoffst, dass es nicht regnet.
- Du findest es schade, dass ihr am Freitag in die Schule gehen müsst.
- Sage, dass du Kassetten lieber hast als Schallplatten.
- Bedaure, dass das Wetter so schlecht ist.

- (Dein Freund möchte ins Schwimmbad gehen.) Mache einen Gegenvorschlag: Du willst ins Kino.
- Bitte deine Freunde in deinem Zimmer nicht zu rauchen.
- Sage, dass deiner Meinung nach die Probe zu schwierig war.
- Wünsche deiner Schwester einen schönen Urlaub.
- Frage deinen Onkel, ob er sich für Tennis interessiert.
- Sage, dass dir der Film „..." (ein aktueller Kinofirlm) sehr gut gefallen hast und du ihn zweimal gesehen hast.
- Bitte deine Freundin, eine Stunde später zu kommen.

Übung 12: Übungen zur Grammatik

- Zeigen Sie jetzt, ob Sie die Grammatik anwenden können. Kopieren und vergrößern Sie diese Seite auf ein DIN-A4-Blatt. Schreiben Sie die richtige Pluralform daneben. Achtung! Bei einigen Wörtern ist das schwierig.

umbrella	_____	test	_____	van	_____
vegetable	_____	waiter	_____	week	_____
secretary	_____	park	_____	race	_____
raincoat	_____	stomach	_____	city	_____
cushion	_____	witch	_____	date	_____
assistant	_____	airport	_____	ashtray	_____
camera	_____	furniture	_____	licence	_____
match	_____	photo	_____	present	_____
window	_____	order	_____	opposite	_____
lamp	_____	machine	_____	money	_____
shower	_____	smoke	_____	wife	_____

Übung 13 zur unregelmäßigen Steigerung

- Im Kasten sind Adjektive versteckt. Schreiben Sie diese heraus und steigern sie. Achten Sie auf die Schreibweise.

> fcleverieunbadoeieuyxmbusyfpoyxmlittlefpoiyxmnarrowfpeangry-
> fpmslowpzxmoldfummuchfiemnicefidboringfßsmallfpousefulfpom-
> coldaiegoodfpieyoungfpoieinuuyxmfamousfaposieienearfuveieuyxmfaruve

_____

_____

_____

_____

Übung 14: Fragen bilden

- Kopieren und vergrößern Sie diese Seite auf ein DIN-A4-Blatt. Bilden Sie zu den Antworten die Fragesätze. Manchmal gibt es auch mehrere Möglichkeiten.

Who plays the trumpet?   *John plays the trumpet.*
oder: *What does John play?*

_____   *He arrived yesterday.*

_____   *Janet wrote a letter.*

_____   *No, I'm at home.*

_____   *I didn't call you.*

_____   *He knows a lot.*

_____   *Richard speaks German.*

_____   *You can do it.*

_____   *I would do something.*

_____   *It's raining.*

_____   *They are going to London tomorrow.*

_____   *You mustn't play tennis.*

_____   *It's Peter's car.*

_____   *Jürgen is at home.*

_____   *Mary is laughing because it's funny.*

_____   *I decorated my room yesterday.*

_____   *Nobody saw me.*

_____   *Mr Smith bought it yesterday.*

_____   *Jennifer got a cold.*

_____   *The 7.30 train goes to London.*

Übung 15: **Weitere Übungen zur englischen Grammatik**

- Jetzt kann man zeigen, ob man einige Teile der englischen Grammatik beherrscht. Kopieren und vergrößern Sie diese Seite auf ein DIN-A4-Blatt. Übersetzen Sie die folgenden Sätze.

1. Meine Eltern sind sehr jung. – Ich brauche eine neue Brille. – Diese Nachricht ist wirklich interessant.

_____

_____

2. Gestern war ich in der Disco. Heute gehe ich ins Kino. Morgen möchte ich gerne schwimmen.

_____

_____

3. Dieses Haus ist schön, das Hotel dort ist schöner, am schönsten aber ist das Schloss. – Heute ist das Wetter schlecht. Gestern war es aber noch schlechter. Am letzten Samstag war es am schlechtesten.

_____

_____

_____

4. Mein Onkel trinkt ein Glas Bier. – Die Jacke von Katja ist rot.

_____

5. „Dein Fahrrad ist wirklich gut", sagt Hans zu Frank. Fritz fragt seinen Lehrer: „Wie ist Ihr Fahrrad?" Herr Maier meint: „Meines ist besser, aber alle unsere Fahrräder sind gut, oder?"

_____

_____

_____

6. „Ich mache das am besten selbst", antwortet Jochen.

_____